Research as a Basis for Teaching

readings from the work of
Lawrence Stenhouse

ABOUT THE EDITORS

Jean Rudduck is Professor of Education at the University of Sheffield. She previously worked as a member of staff at the Centre for Applied Research in Education at the University of East Anglia, as a member of the Humanities Curriculum Project central team, and as a teacher.

David Hopkins is currently a lecturer in educational research at the West Glamorgan Institute of Higher Education, Swansea. He previously worked as a lecturer in the Faculty of Education at Simon Fraser University, Canada, as a teacher in the West Riding of Yorkshire, and (still) as a mountain guide.

Research as a Basis for Teaching

*readings from the work of
Lawrence Stenhouse*

edited by

*Jean Rudduck
and David Hopkins*

Heinemann Educational Books · London · Portsmouth (NH)

Heinemann Educational Books Ltd
22 Bedford Square, London WC1B 3HH
Heinemann Educational Books Inc
70 Court Street, Portsmouth, New Hampshire 03801

LONDON   EDINBURGH   MELBOURNE   AUCKLAND
HONG KONG   SINGAPORE   KUALA LUMPUR   NEW DELHI
IBADAN   NAIROBI   JOHANNESBURG
PORTSMOUTH (NH)   KINGSTON   PORT OF SPAIN

First published 1985

British Library Cataloguing in Publication Data

Stenhouse Lawrence
  Research as a basis for teaching: readings from the work of Lawrence Stenhouse
  1. Teaching   2. Education — Research
  I. Title II. Rudduck, Jean III. Hopkins, David, *1949-*
  371.1 '0072   LB1028

  ISBN 0-435-80785-4

Library of Congress Cataloging in Publication Data

Stenhouse, Lawrence.
  Research as a basis for teaching.

  "Select bibliography of the work of
Lawrence Stenhouse": p. 131
  1. Education——Research——Great Britain. 2. Curriculum planning——Great Britain. 3. Teaching. I. Rudduck, Jean. II. Hopkins, David. III. Title.

  LB1028.S7953   1985   370 '.7 '8041   84-28989
  ISBN 0-435-80785-4

Typeset by the Castlefield Press, Northampton,
and printed in Great Britain by Biddles Ltd, Guildford

Contents

'It is teachers who, in the end,
will change the world of the school
by understanding it.'

A quotation from Lawrence Stenhouse, chosen by some of the
teachers who worked with him as an inscription for the memorial
plaque in the grounds of the University of East Anglia.

Acknowledgements

We would like to thank all those who granted permission to reproduce material listed on the copyright page of this book, and also Harry Torrance for allowing us to use the dialogue with Lawrence Stenhouse.

Editors' note

Many of the extracts reproduced in this book are inconsistent with current conventions regarding the use of the personal pronoun. However, we have decided to leave the passages as they are and instead to reprint the 'apology' that Lawrence Stenhouse himself made to explain why he had not altered the original texts of the papers that he included in his book *Authority, Education and Emancipation*. He wrote 'I am sufficiently sensitive to the sexist use of language, particularly blatant in some of the earlier papers, to feel the desire to offer my apologies to all readers who for "he" must read "she", and my regrets to readers of whichever sex.' these are sentiments that we share.

Introduction

'Research as a basis for teaching' was the title of the inaugural lecture that Lawrence Stenhouse gave, in February 1979, at the University of East Anglia. Readers will probably interpret the title in terms of the 'teacher as researcher' movement but in the lecture he examined the relationship between teaching and research in universities as well as in schools.

It was in his work with schools, however, that the principles that inform this relationship were most systematically explored. They were first given practical expression in the experimental pedagogy of the Humanities Curriculum Project. John Elliott, a member of the Project team, commented recently on what he thought was distinctive in the approach: 'What Stenhouse offered teachers . . . was a curriculum conceived as a set of hypothetical procedures they could experiment with as a basis for the reflective translation of educational ideas into educational actions' (1983: 108–9).

Lawrence Stenhouse expected teachers to be tentative, sceptical and experimental in their engagement with the Project, and the trust that he had in teachers helped many to establish a new professionalism – which Barry Macdonald, the Project's evaluator, described in this way: 'The promise was a future in which from a process of redefinition of the relationship between teachers, taught and knowledge . . . teachers (would be transformed) into research-based master craftsmen of a new tradition' (1976: 81).

In 1970 Lawrence Stenhouse and some of his colleagues on the Humanities Project moved from London to the University of East Anglia and, while the Project was still in progress, established the Centre for Applied Research in Education (CARE). A common concern of the Centre staff was to demystify and democratize research, which was seen as failing to contribute effectively to the growth of professional understanding and to the improvement of professional practice. One possible explanation of this failure was the reluctance of educational researchers to engage teachers as partners in, and critics of, the research process. Many teachers, as a consequence, have an ambivalent attitude towards research, some according it too much respect, uncritically; others dismissing its findings without proper scrutiny. It is important therefore for researchers to accept that the propositions they offer teachers are unlikely to affect practice if their warrant lies in the expertise of persons or methodologies rather than in the appeal they make to professional experience and judgement.

In Lawrence Stenhouse's next major curriculum project, teachers from participating schools were explicitly cast as 'internal researchers' and the university-based team as 'external researchers'. The project was called – with a characteristic underlining of its non-prescriptive stance – 'The Problems and Effects of Teaching about Race Relations' (1972–5). He maintained that it is the responsibility of the university researcher to speculate rather than instruct, and the project report ends (somewhat perversely it must seem to people who are unfamiliar with the logic of his position) with a set of hypotheses. The hypotheses are in fact a point of transition, where the project hands on the research task to an audience of teachers who can test the hypotheses – which were distilled from a careful analysis of case-study data and data from a measurement programme – through experiment in the particular settings of their own classrooms and schools.

Various colleagues who worked at the Centre in the seventies designed projects which closely involved teachers in the definition of the research task and in the gathering and analysis of data from their own classrooms (most notably John Elliott and Clem Adelman in the Ford Teaching Project). Thus, through a series of research projects which addressed significant problems in curriculum and pedagogy, the teacher as researcher movement was given identity and credibility.

But CARE was a teaching centre as well as a research centre and if it had a slogan that united the two activities it was the title of this book – research as a basis for teaching. Research conducted by members of the Centre staff and by students in their own classrooms has been the backbone of the taught Master's courses. The strength of this approach – for which we paid the price of a certain insularity – is that research holds knowledge problematic and protects students, experienced teachers and advisers from the trap of wanting to be told and then believing what they are told.

Our aim in this book is to bring together passages from Lawrence Stenhouse's talks and writing that document his view of research and his argument for making research a basis for teaching. Taking his work as a whole, there is a remarkable continuity of concern, reaching back to the essays he wrote for his degree in education and forward into the last project he directed in which he and his colleagues tried to throw light on the role of the library in the crucial transition, for students, from dependence on instruction to capacity for autonomous thinking (see Rudduck and Hopkins, 1984). Indeed, all his work was distinguished by a deep-rooted curiosity about the relationship between authority and knowledge. He said, of schooling: 'We produce through education a majority who are ruled by knowledge, not served by it – an intellectual, moral and spiritual proletariat characterized by instrumental competencies rather than autonomous power' (1978).

The responsibility of teachers, at all levels, is to free students from the insularity of their own minds, prevent them from lodging in the comfortable branches of the teacher's thought, and to try instead to foster a less cautious and confined exploration of knowledge: one that confers on those who seek it, in a spirit of critical enquiry, the power of its use. This was the commitment that gave energy to his curriculum work for schools and to his teaching.

In a lecture to the Dartington Conference (1978) Lawrence Stenhouse took as his theme an 'old-fashioned' concept – emancipation – and this, we believe, is the central concept in his work – the key that unlocks the pattern of his thinking. In the lecture he went on to say: 'The essence of emancipation as I conceive it is the . . . autonomy which we recognize when we eschew paternalism and the role of authority and hold ourselves obliged to appeal to judgement.'

One route to emancipation is for the teacher to adopt the perspective of the researcher: the teacher-researcher role is, therefore, a means to an end rather than an end in itself. This argument rests on two principles: first, that teacher research is linked to the strengthening of teacher judgement and consequently to the self-directed improvement of practice; second, that the most important focus for research is the curriculum in that it is the medium through which knowledge is communicated in schools. Accepting this logic, we divided the book into two main sections, one on Lawrence Stenhouse's view of research and one on his view of curriculum.

Despite the accessibility of Lawrence's material, this has not been an easy book to prepare – partly because of our closeness to Lawrence and his ideas and partly because he is an extremely difficult writer to anthologize. He is a little like the Welsh fundamentalist preacher of whom it was said: 'Many, many are the texts, but all the sermons one'. He had a similarly compulsive zest. And since he wrote and spoke in many different settings to many different audiences, one finds the same set of ideas being re-examined and moved forward – almost like

progressive elaborations in a Bach fugue. Our problem was of putting
the case strongly but without undue repetition, and this meant that we
could not use too many of his papers whole. Yet he is a dynamic and
stylish writer and it is difficult to cut into the argument to extract
chunks of prose. Indeed, one referee for the book warned us against
'over-zealous editing'. 'Good writing is', he claimed, 'organic, not
atomistic: when you cut it, it bleeds'. We have had to edit, but we have
taken the warning to heart.

When Susan Sontag was preparing a book of readings from the
work of Roland Barthes she had four criteria for selecting passages:
passages were chosen because they seemed 'representative' of his
thinking; because they had been 'influential' on the thinking of
others; and because they had appealed to her personally as either
'particularly fortifying' or 'irresistibly odd' (1982: xxxvii). We were in
sympathy with this blend of public and private criteria. We first
selected papers that presented the main contours of Lawrence
Stenhouse's thinking, and then chose passages from them that we
considered characteristically energetic in their stalking of powerful
ideas and characteristically striking in their articulation of those ideas.
We also tried to include passages that reflected something of the
peculiar tension in his writing between stylistic robustness on the one
hand and an intellectual commitment to uncertainty on the other – not
that this tension implies a contradiction, for although he tried to
produce convincing arguments, he did so from a position of genuine
openness. He wanted people to appreciate his ideas, said a local
teacher, but always as a result of argument and never through mere
deference. Indeed, he could be a tiger in debate, but less to score
points than to evoke an intelligent criticism that would help him to see
new ways of exploring or expressing an idea. Readers of this book will
have to take responsibility themselves for challenging his thinking
and putting a counter-argument. And it is important that they do so
for, to paraphrase one of his own statements, ideas become
stereotyped or derelict when they cease to develop. As D.H.
Lawrence wrote in an introduction to a collection of his poetry which
he called *Pansies* (i.e. 'Pensées' or 'Thoughts'): 'I offer a bunch of
pansies, not a wreath of immortelles. I don't want everlasting flowers'.

We should perhaps say a little more about our editorial work. After
much deliberation we decided to exercise our creativity in the
selection and juxtaposition of extracts rather than in editorial
comment, believing that Lawrence Stenhouse was well able to speak
for himself and that explication would be gratuitous. In sequencing
the passages we have tried to construct an argument; we think that the
argument will become increasingly clear as readers move through the

book but brief signposts are given at the start of the three sections. Each section is introduced by a paper, reproduced in full, that raises many of the key issues and gives the reader a sense of the way that Lawrence Stenhouse structured and handled his own argument. Thereafter issues are developed and illustrated in a series of subsections, through extracts of varying length. The book ends with the reproduction, in full, of the lecture from which it takes its title, 'Research as a basis for teaching'.

Lawrence Stenhouse died in September 1982, in mid-intellectual career. Nevertheless he leaves a legacy of powerful ideas which we have tried to gather and order in a way that make them accessible but that does not overly predetermine the meanings the reader can make with them. Many threads are left untied, but whatever is unfinished leaves space for others to work in.

References

ELLIOTT, J. (1983) A curriculum for the study of human affairs: the contribution of Lawrence Stenhouse *Journal of Curriculum Studies* 15, 2, 105–23.

LAWRENCE, D.H. (1929) *Pansies* Martin Secker.

MACDONALD, B. and WALKER, R. (1976) *Changing the Curriculum* Open Books.

RUDDUCK, J. and HOPKINS, D. (1984) *The Sixth Form and Libraries: Problems of Access to Knowledge* British Library.

SONTAG, S. (ed.) (1982) *Barthes: Selected Writings* Fontana/Collins.

STENHOUSE, L. 'Towards a vernacular humanism': paper given at the Dartington Conference, 1978, and published in L. Stenhouse (1983) *Authority, Education and Emancipation* Heinemann Educational Books.

STENHOUSE, L. (with VERMA, G.K., WILD, R.D. and NIXON, J.) (1982) *Teaching about Race Relations: Problems and Effects* Routledge & Kegan Paul.

Section 1

Research

Research, to be of use to teachers, requires that they test its theoretical implications in their classrooms. Much educational research, because of its allegiance to the psycho-statistical paradigm, expresses its findings as generalizations that cannot claim to offer guidance for action in particular settings. More supportive of teacher practice is research that either issues in hypotheses that can be tested in classrooms or that illuminates particular cases that can be judged against experience. Both can provide a stimulus to the planning of research-based enquiry in classrooms. Teachers who want to initiate research can appropriately employ an action-research framework as a means of discovering hypotheses whose testing can lead to the improvement of practice and serve as an alternative route to the generation of theory.

J.R. & D.H.

WHAT COUNTS AS RESEARCH*

I shall begin by hazarding a minimal definition: research is systematic self-critical enquiry.

As an enquiry, it is founded in curiosity and a desire to understand; but it is a stable, not a fleeting, curiosity, systematic in the sense of being sustained by a strategy. When Jane Goodall confronted a chimpanzee with a looking-glass, the animal, after gesticulating at its own image, felt behind the glass in order – may I say loosely – to understand the situation; but after a few moments it passed on to other activities. Not so the researcher, who has bred a persistence of sequential enquiry by curiosity out of patience. And fundamental to such persistence of enquiry is a sceptical temper of mind sustained by critical principles, a doubt not only about the received and comfortable answers, but also about one's own hypotheses.

The research spirit is displayed in Thucydides, Peter Abélard, Galileo, Samuel Johnson, David Hume, George Stubbs, Charles Darwin, Max Weber, Igor Stravinsky and James Joyce – to name only an historian, a theologian, a physicist, a lexicographer, a philosopher, a painter, a biologist, a social scientist, a musician and a novelist. But a list of such names gives research a Promethean cast: they are the saints and martyrs of the research calendar. Research nowadays is an every-day activity: an industry, a tool and a pastime. Where Icarus fell, the Boeing now carries the linguist with a research problem in Middle Eastern dialects, the business man with a commission to research Middle Eastern markets, the novelist researching the Middle Eastern setting of his next novel and the antique collector trying to build context round his small collection of Middle Eastern earthenware.

It was not always so. People with questions and problems turned – as many still do – to answers from divine revelation, to the authority of a learned caste, to traditional lore or the received opinion. And curiosity is as ever dangerous, because it leads to intellectual innovation which brings in its trail a press towards social change. To those who yearn for the support of faith, authority and tradition, research presents a threat of heresy. Yet without the organized pursuit of curiosity we could not sustain our social life.

The utility of research generally brings to people's minds the hard science that lies behind their kitchen equipment or television, but my

* What counts as research? *British Journal of Educational Studies* 29, 2, June 1981

homeland is history and so, like Carl Becker (1931) or Jacques Barzun and Henry Graff (1977), I see history as the archetypal utilitarian research. Barzun and Graff call it 'the Great Catch-All'. It lies behind our recipe books rather than our cooking pots. While the hard sciences produce our hardware, history produces our software: it is the expression of a systematic critical enquiry into the fruits of our experience. In the broadest sense the physical and life sciences pursue research into the *context* of experience: history is concerned – again in the broadest sense – with research into the *content* of experience.

You will be clear that I am not using the term *history* in the narrow sense sometimes adopted in schools and universities. Like those authors to whom I have made reference I am distinguishing between the researches of science, which characteristically seek laws or theories not narrowly conditional upon time, and those researches cast in a historical perspective, which recognize time as an essential variable in the accounts they give. Once we are in time there is no account of the present. As Barzun and Graff (1977: 5) note, 'description of "the present" is actually a description of the past – recent it may be, but nonetheless a backward glance.' Both science and history are given to generalization – in spite of the disclaimers of some historians – but science aspires to generalizations which are predictive and universal, whereas historical generalization is retrospective and summarizes experience within boundaries of time and place.

The position I have sketched is clearly problematic at many points, but I must be highly selective in the problems I take up. Since all are united – I assume – by an interest in the relevance of research to the practical activity of education, I must ask some questions about the relevance of science and history to practice, and, by implication, to future practice. And I can only sketch some answers to these questions. Then, I must look at the 'human sciences' of psychology and sociology to locate them in the wider picture of research. Finally, I shall turn to the problems of values and interests in research.

I have, I must confess, withheld to this point a problem concerning my simple definition of research, which I now bring out into the open by quoting a headline from Barzun and Graff: 'The Historical Attitude Underlies *Research* and *Report*'. In a previous paper (Stenhouse, 1979) I described research as 'systematic enquiry *made public*'. What is the role of report in research? What is the status of research-based action? What is the relation of report to discourse and to practice? These questions, as well as those set out in the previous paragraph, deserve at least a glance before I turn to the practical problem which I have assumed to be the hidden agenda lying between the lines of the letter inviting me to contribute this paper: what credible force can we give to the slogan, *Teacher as Researcher?*

The Relevance of Science and History to Practice

Scientists attempt to account for consistencies of occurrence or of the conjunction of occurrences over time or for events which are regarded as inevitable outcomes of preceding causes. Or, to put it another way, scientists are interested in the power of laws and theories which are general and predictive to organize and summarize data derived from observations. Whether or not the laws of science are invented by mind or discovered in nature, together with many other controversies, need not concern us for the moment.

The first and most obvious application of science to practice rests on the capacity of predictions to provide us with information about the context of action. To put it crudely, I can plan my farming on the prediction that there will be seasons, or my navigation on the prediction that there will be tides. Such predictions do not guide me by telling me exactly what to do, though they may tell me fairly clearly what I should not do. A simple way to express them is to say that they set the conditions of the game: they are the field of play and perhaps the rules in their barest form.

The second application of science to practice works through the possibility of applying general laws to the problem of predicting the outcomes of specific acts. This enables me to design acts on the basis of a more or less reliable estimate of their outcome: to calculate that my bridge will stand or that my glue will stick.

These two applications of science strengthen, but do not supersede, common sense. Nor do they tell us whether to build our bridge, for all that they predict the traffic flows and assure us that we can construct a bridge that will stand.

History has an application close to the first application of science suggested above. It helps to define the conditions of action by summarizing experience in such a way as to suggest the considerations we shall have to take into account as we make judgements as to how to act. We must attempt to understand the complex web of social variables which contextualize our actions and influence the outcomes. Historical analyses which support such understanding are more useful across time than is sometimes recognized: the speeches arguing for and against war in Thucydides' history of the Peloponnesian War are no bad introduction to an understanding of the ground rules of the present conflict between Iran and Iraq. Judgements of relevance to our acting in any given case can be founded on such stocktaking, 'state-of-the-nation' reports, which are 'contemporary histories' in the sense that they are accounts of a past as close to our present – or perhaps, better said, to our future – as we can make them.

History is also able to summarize the experience of action in such a way as to strengthen judgement and revision of judgement in planning acts. It enables us to make judgemental predictions of how events will go and to revise those predictions in the face of surprise by rapid reassessments. Paradoxically, history both predicts that events will be substantially unpredictable and supports our attempts to narrow the bounds of unpredictability both by judgemental predictions and by contingency plans. Further, it offers to make us adept at reading the significance of the unexpected and reacting shrewdly to it. It helps us to play what, by analogy with chess, we may call 'the middle game'.

Science and history have a great deal more in common than is sometimes believed: both help to define the context in which people act, and both help to anticipate the outcomes of actions. But when we apply science, we premise high predictability, and when we apply history we premise low predictability. I believe that the acts and thoughts of individual human beings contain essential unpredictable elements owing to the human capacity for creative problem-solving and the creation of meanings. Others, of course, will see unpredictability in human action as the wilderness beyond the advancing frontier of a social science, a wilderness to be colonized in the future.

Social Science and Practice

Although social science begins with an attempt to apply the methods of natural science to social phenomena in the confidence that human action is lawfully predictable, it would be quite unjust to burden contemporary social science with this heritage. In practice, experimental and analytic social science seeks to ride the assumption of high predictability as far as it may, while observational and naturalistic social science attempts to work in areas where the assumption of low predictability seems stronger. There is nothing ultimately contradictory in nibbling that bit of string from both ends.

The application of the work of the analytic experimentalists to practice is at two levels, corresponding broadly to two research traditions. A laboratory tradition seeks general laws and theories which are analogous to those in certain areas of the natural sciences. The area of learning theory is a good example of this kind of work. Concepts such as recency, frequency, reinforcement, proactive and retroactive inhibition and so forth are pretty well anchored and contribute to synthetic theory. In my view the interest of this kind of work is currently underestimated by educators, but its relevance to practice is rather in defining ground rules than in discriminating action. It draws attention to some of the variables at work in a complex multi-variate situation, but it does not enable us to predict outcomes in such situations.

It is in part this shortcoming which presses the social scientist to come out of the laboratory and undertake field research of a kind which faces real situations with their full multi-variate complexity. Quasi-experimental designs (Campbell and Stanley, 1963) are applied directly to practice, usually to attempt to predict the effects of actions, the crucial tools being the statistical procedures which allow estimates of reliability, of internal and external validity, and the use of analysis of variance and correlated techniques. This tradition of field experiment in which Galton and Fisher are key figures fails to discriminate the effects of specific actions on specific cases (Hamilton, 1980). What it yields are indications of trends, that is, actuarial predictions for populations; and often in educational research these predictions suffer from weak external validity. For example, Bennett's work on *Teaching Styles and Pupil Progress* (1976) fails to control the LEA as a variable, while the Humanities Project experiment in teaching style revealed the LEA as a crucial factor. Moreover, when it comes to the problem of how to act as an individual teacher in the light of the Bennett research, it is not clear whether one should adopt the formal style which gave the best mean results or the informal style which gave an excellent, perhaps the best, single result.

In short, it seems that while social science applied to education can produce results which help us to understand the ground rules of action, it cannot provide the basis for a technology of teaching which offers reliable guidance to the teacher. Predictions based upon statistical levels of confidence are applicable to action only when the same treatment must be given throughout the entire population. This condition does not apply in education. It is the teacher's task to differentiate treatments.

It is in part the recognition of this problem that accounts for the spread of interest in naturalistic or ethnographic styles of educational research. The portrayal of cases offers to inform the judgement of actors – the administrators, teachers, pupils or parents – rather after the manner of history, by opening the research accounts to recognition and to comparison and hence to criticism in the light of experience. Such a refinement of experienced practical judgement eludes the psycho-statistical model which strips the data of recognizable characteristics and context, and presents 'findings' or 'results' which are accessible to criticism only by replication or by technical attack on the design or conduct of the research.

However, naturalistic styles of social research, in contrast to laboratory or field experiments, do appear to accept real time as a dimension and the question arises: is naturalistic research simply and necessarily history?

To my mind the extent to which naturalistic studies should draw on the traditions of history or of social science is one of the most important issues in contemporary social research. I have written elsewhere on the topic and this is not the place to explore it at length. But one issue has central relevance here: the status of theory.

History, though not wholly atheoretical, is nonetheless parsimonious of theory. In particular, the historian points up issues as often by ambiguity as by stating hypotheses. Since his account is not conspicuously theoretical, the historian takes most of his terms of art from his subjects. Thus, the historian of parliament will use the terms of parliamentarians, the historian of music, the terms of musicians, and so forth. One great strength of history is that its vocabulary is accessible to those who are interested in the topic under discussion.

Social scientists, even naturalistic social scientists, appear to be much more interested in theory than are historians. Even when they are not hotly in pursuit of laws they still have a taste for theory, for they seek generalizations which go across the boundaries of human interests and hence of interest-linked vocabularies. They are, to simplify the matter a little, interested in human and social and political behaviour rather than the behaviour of parliamentarians or musicians or beekeepers or teachers. Social scientists themselves are a group with their own language (which others often criticize as jargon) which not only arranges their world so that they can communicate with one another, but also relates discourse to actions. But the act to which the discourse relates is primarily the social science research act. The discipline of social science, expressed in the language of social science, organizes social science knowledge in such a way as to point up promising lines of research and organizes understanding of methodology and method to support the planning of the research act. To apply social science to teaching most often requires a translation and one difficult enough for researchers to yearn for a richer literacy of the consumer.

The question arises: could we have an educational science? It is a question that can be construed in many ways, but here I mean: could we have a study of educational phenomena which opted neither for the common language of education nor for the language of social science theory, but instead for a theory which related directly to educational practice? Not a sociology, nor a psychology, but a pedagogy.

For the moment, I shall leave that question hanging.

Values and Interests in Research

I need to take up the issue of objectivity in social research, and it is not an issue I am well equipped to handle, partly because I personally have been untroubled by the problem. I am content that human and social research (and probably also all research that is interested in interpretation or theory rather than mere brute facts) should aim to ground discourse in dependable intersubjectivities. For me disciplines of knowlege or complexes of research are founded on 'arrests of experience' (Oakeshott, 1933), limitations of aspiration which allow us to order experience within conditional boundaries. To name something is, in any event, to make it accessible to discussion at the expense of both oversimplifying it and rendering it ambiguous.

It is commonplace that research is attacked on the grounds that the researcher has allowed an intrusion of his values. It will help my analysis, as well as suit my inclinations, if I consider the perspectives given to research not by the researcher's values but by his interest. I use the word *interest* in two dictionary senses which are clearly related: 'being concerned or affected in respect of advantage or detriment' and 'feeling of concern for or curiosity about a person or thing'. Now it is clear that the second of those definitions accords pretty closely with what I have suggested is the impulse behind all research – curiosity – and I believe that such curiosity is almost inevitably associated with considerations of advantage or detriment.

In particular, it should be noted, interest figures prominently in applied sciences: we build a bridge because it is advantageous to us to do so and that advantage breeds a curiosity about bridges. Moreover, the building of a good bridge is to our advantage not only in the primary sense that it lets us cross the river, but also in the secondary sense that successful achievement rewards us in terms of reputation, material payment and future opportunities. In most cases these interests do not impel us to falsify our formulae and build bridges that fall down. The collapse of a bridge is difficult to hide: we do not fudge our process when it is impossible to falsify our result.

The prime problem of interests (and values) in research is this: when the tests of our hypotheses or interpretations are not rigorous, there is a temptation to make dubious claims which appear likely to promote our reputation, increase our material rewards, better our future prospects or endorse some policy to which we are devoted independently of the research.

All researchers are beset by temptations of interest which may blow them off course. The crucial problem is the strength of the critical process which controls such temptations, and such a critical process is essentially social as well as methodological. The case of Cyril Burt is instructive. The person who is too powerful to be questioned – like the person who is too clever to be understood – cannot be controlled by the adoption of methods which purport to support objectivity.

Enquiry counts as research to the extent that it is systematic, but even more to the extent that it can claim to be conscientiously self-critical.

The Teacher-Researcher

The basic argument for placing teachers at the heart of the educational research process may be simply stated. Teachers are in charge of classrooms. From the point of view of the experimentalist, classrooms are the ideal laboratories for the testing of educational theory. From the point of view of the researcher whose interest lies in naturalistic observation, the teacher is a potential participant observer in classrooms and schools. From whatever standpoint we view research, we must find it difficult to deny that the teacher is surrounded by rich research opportunities.

Moreover, there is in the research field of education little theory which could be relied upon by the teacher without testing it. Many of the findings of research are based on small-scale or laboratory experiments which often do not replicate or cannot be successfully applied in classrooms. Many are actuarial and probabilistic, and, if they are to be used by the individual teacher, they demand situational verification. The application of insights drawn from naturalistic case studies to a teacher's situation rests upon the quality of the teacher's study of his home case. Using research means doing research. The teacher has grounds for motivation to research. We researchers have reason to excite that motivation: without a research response from teachers our research cannot be utilized.

And, after all, much medical research even in universities is conducted by practitioner-researchers. We pay them more and call them clinical.

There are, however, a number of objections to the teacher as a researcher.

First, it is said that tests of the accuracy of teachers' self-reports suggest that teachers do not know what they do. Although this shortcoming can be exaggerated, it has substance. A teacher lays the foundation of his capacity for research by developing self-monitoring strategies. The effect is not unlike that of making the transition from amateur to professional actor. Through self-monitoring the teacher becomes a conscious artist. Through conscious art he is able to use himself as an instrument of his research.

Second, it is claimed that involvement in the action of school and classroom gives teachers an interest in the tendency of research findings and condemns them to bias. This is not in my view a sustainable objection. In my experience the dedication of professional researchers to their theories is a more serious source of bias than the dedication of teachers to their practice. Teachers whose work I have examined at master's and doctoral level seem to me to achieve remarkably cool and dispassionate appraisals. I see more distortion produced by academic battles than by practical concerns. But I must concede that there are forbidden areas for most teacher-researchers and that these are mainly where the exposure of persons and personal relationships is at stake. In general, however, the professional researcher seems to me more vulnerable because of his distance from practice and his lack of responsibility for practice than is the teacher by virtue of his involvement in practice.

Researchers sometimes regard teachers as theoretically innocent. But much professional research drawing on, if not feeding, the disciplines is also theoretically innocent. This is true of most surveys, field experiments and evaluations. You can partly detect them by the sign that all the theoretical work of their authors is methodological. On the other hand, some teachers are theorists, hot from Ph.Ds or having informally developed theoretical interests. What teachers most often lack is confidence and experience in relating theory to design and in the conduct of research work.

The most serious impediment to the development of teachers as researchers – and indeed as artists in teaching – is quite simply shortage of time. In this country teachers teach too much. So research by teachers is a minority activity, commonly stimulated and supported by formal degree structures at master's and doctoral level, or by participation in a research project with the teacher-research concept built in. In rare persons the interest and activity is sustained. In a number of cases teacher research develops as someone turns to immersion in work as a response to bereavement or other crises. Much clearly needs to be done to ameliorate the burdens of the teacher prepared to embark on a programme of research and development.

Publication
Earlier in this paper I mentioned that a full definition of research might include the qualification that it be made public. Private re-

search for our purpose does not count as research. Partly, this is because unpublished research does not profit by criticism. Partly, it is because we see research as a community effort and unpublished research is of little use to others. What seems to me most important is that research becomes part of a community of critical discourse. But perhaps too much research is published to the world, too little to the village. We need local cooperatives and papers as well as international conferences and journals. And in any case we need more face-to-face discourse. It's a pity, perhaps, that in this country the doctorate is not publicly defended.

Here is a description of a particular model of a critical community (Gramsci, 1967):

> One type of deliberative college which seeks to incorporate the necessary technical competence to work realistically has been described elsewhere, where I spoke of what happens on the editorial boards of certain reviews, which function as cultural circles at the same time as editorial boards. The circle criticizes in a collegiate way and so contributes towards developing the work of individual members of the editorial staff whose own task is organized according to a rationally worked out plan and division of labour.

> Through discussion and joint criticisms (consisting of suggestions, advice, indications of method, constructive criticism directed towards mutual learning), by which each man functions as a specialist in his own subject to improve the collective competence, the average level of each individual is raised. It reaches the height or the capacity of the best trained and assures the review not only of ever better selected and organic contributions but creates the conditions for the rise of a homogeneous group of intellectuals trained to produce regular and methodical literary activity (not only in *livres d'occasion* and partial studies, but in organic general works as well).

> Undoubtedly in this kind of collective activity each job produces the capacity and possibility for new work, since it creates even more organic conditions of work: card indexes, bibliographical notes, collections of basic specialized works, etc. A rigorous struggle is required against habits of dilettantism, improvisation, oratorical and declamatory solutions. It is important for reports, and this applies to criticisms, to be made in written form in short succinct notes. This can be ensured by distributing material in good time etc. Writing notes and criticisms is a didactic principle rendered necessary by the need to combat habits of prolixity, declamation and sophistry created by oratory . . . .

Publication has two functions. It opens work to criticism and consequently to refinement; and it also disseminates the fruits of research and hence makes possible the cumulation of knowledge. When systematic enquiry is shared in groups whose character approximates Gramsci's deliberative college, it enjoys the advantage of criticism, but it does not necessarily disseminate outside the collegiate group. Work undertaken in such a context must, in my view, count as research. Indeed, the critical process in the group might with advantage act as a filter. If publication were more selective, we might be in less danger of cumulating the redundant or ephemeral.

There is, however, a less obvious implication of Gramsci's idea. His deliberative college is dedicated to action (in this case running a newspaper). In this it might be compared to a school or teachers' centre group or to an opera company or to a cooperative workshop. The question arises: can research be expressed in performances or actions? I think it can if its force is to make action hypothetical or problematic. To the extent that a substantive action is an expression of a research enquiry, it tests the hypothetical outcome of the enquiry; and this is one understanding of action research.

Alongside our received academic notion of what constitutes publication, we must, I think, allow that research can find other utterances – in critical groups or in action – which can be subject to disciplines which test its claims. Indeed, it could be a weakness of much research in education that it is insufficiently tested in action, too readily accepted by its mere survival in the academic debate.

What Counts as Educational Research?

Research, I have suggested, is systematic and sustained enquiry, planned and self-critical, which is subjected to public criticism and to empirical tests where these are appropriate. Where empirical tests are not appropriate, critical discourse will appeal to judgement of evidence – the test, the document, the observation, the record. In applied or action research the test or evidence may be provided by substantive action, that is, action which must be justified in other than research terms.

I conclude by asking: what counts as research in education? I mean by research *in* education, research conducted within the educational intention and contributory to the educational enterprise. There is, of course, in history, philosophy, psychology and sociology, research *on* education conducted from the standpoint of the disciplines which contributes to the educational enterprise incidentally if at all. It is, one might say, educational research only in the sense that Durkheim gave us suicidal research.

Research is educational to the extent that it can be related to the practice of education. Whether this relationship is to be made by a theory of pedagogy at some level of generalization or by an extension of experience which informs practice or by providing the framework for action research as a tool to explore the characteristics of particular situations or by critical evaluation of practice, or by all of these, appears an open question. But two points seem to me clear: first, teachers must inevitably be intimately involved in the research process; and second, researchers must justify themselves to practitioners, not practitioners to researchers.

References

BARZUN, J. and GRAFF, H.F. (1977, 3rd edition) *The Modern Researcher* New York: Harcourt Brace Jovanovich.

BECKER, C. (1931) 'Everyman his own historian'. Presidential address delivered to the American Historical Association at Minneapolis, 29 December, 1931; reprinted in C. Becker (1966) *Everyman His Own Historian* Chicago: Quadrangle Books. (Original edition New York: Crofts 1935.)

BENNETT, N. (1976) *Teaching Styles and Pupil Progress* Open Books.

CAMPBELL, D. T. and STANLEY, J.C. (1963) 'Experimental and quasi-experimental designs for research on teaching' in N.L. Gage (ed.) *A Handbook of Research on Teaching* Chicago: Rand McNally.

GRAMSCI, A. (1967) 'The organization of education and culture' in *The Modern Prince and Other Writings* New York: International Publishers.

HALPIN, A.W. (1966) *Theory and Research in Administration* Collier/Macmillan.

HAMILTON, D. (1980) 'Educational research and the shadows of Francis Galton and Ronald Fisher' in W.B. Dockrell and D. Hamilton (eds) *Rethinking Educational Research* Hodder and Stoughton.

OAKESHOTT, M. (1933) *Experience and its Modes* Cambridge University Press.

STENHOUSE, L. (1979) 'Research as a basis for teaching', inaugural lecture, University of East Anglia, 1979; published in L. Stenhouse (1983) *Authority, Education and Emancipation* Heinemann Educational Books.

A VIEW OF RESEARCH

The psycho-statistical paradigm and its limitations 1*

Research and evaluation in curriculum and teaching which is conducted in field situations, that is, in real schools and classrooms, is commonly cast in a classic paradigm, which derives from the conduct of experiments in agriculture. The pioneer work in this field is that of R.A. Fisher (1935).

The object of the research design is to enable experiments to be conducted on samples, commonly a control and an experimental, and the results generalized to a target population. If two samples, experimental and control, were so drawn that they were unerringly representative of the target population, then they would be comparable and results on them would hold for the target population. Both internal and external validity would have been achieved. There are no real circumstances which meet this ideal case. In an absolute sense there are no representative samples.

The strength of Fisher's paradigm is the recognition that random sampling, in which a sample is drawn such that each member of the target population has an equal chance of being included in the sample, because it is a device of chance, allows the application of the mathematics of probability. In parametric statistics the assumptions of the normal curve are used as a basis for estimating error, and calculations can be made to quantify the likelihood that experimental and control samples are drawn from the same population. Here the classic paradigm utilizes the null hypothesis.

Logically, this experimental procedure allows us to gamble at stated odds on a substantive hypothesis versus a null hypothesis, the precision of the substantive hypothesis affecting the odds (one-tailed and two-tailed tests).

* From 'Using research means doing research', in H. Dahl, A. Lysne, and P. Rand (eds) *Spotlight on Educational Problems*, Festskrift for Johannes Sandven, Oslo University Press, 1979.

In Fisher's agricultural setting, the hypotheses were not derived from scientific theory to test it. They were hypotheses regarding the relative effectiveness of alternative procedures, and the criterion of effectiveness was gross crop-yield. Block and plot designs were used to randomize the operation of contextual factors such as soil and exposure. Seed strains, fertilizers, watering, etc., were strictly controlled. One variable from this array was controlled for experiment. Yield measures were standardised by measuring only the two rows on a four-row plot. In short, controls were (and are in contemporary agricultural research in this paradigm) very tight indeed.

The result of an experiment of this kind is an estimate of the probability that – other things being equal – a particular seed strain or fertilizer or amount of watering will result in a higher gross yield than an alternative against which it has been tested. Even under the relatively tight controls possible in agricultural research there are problems of generalization due to local variations in soil, climate, rainfall, and so forth. A farmer will often visit an experimental station to weigh up the relation of conditions to his own. Certainly, no standardization of farming practice across the country is possible.

It is important to notice that laboratory experiments in physical sciences, though logically dealing with samples in the Fisherian sense, can often disregard for practical purposes problems of internal and external validity, and use small samples of controlled purity. There are many examples of this style of working in laboratory pyschology.

It is in applying experimental methods to teaching and curriculum evaluation in the schools that researchers have used the Fisherian model. The assumption is that one teaching procedure or curriculum can be tested against alternatives as a seed strain or fertilizer can in agriculture, i.e. procedures can be tested against yield without a real theoretical framework.

There are a number of obvious problems. First, random sampling is not possible nor is it closely approximated; for example a random sample of schools and one of pupils and one of teachers would each have to be drawn separately. Hence, the problems of internal and external validity in educational field experiments considered by Campbell and Stanley (1963) and Snow (1974). Second, the criterion of yield is difficult to establish. The approach to criterion-referenced testing through objectives is either too coarse or fails to produce an agreed measure (Walker and Schaffarzick, 1974). Third, contextual variables muddy our results. It is possible that we might stumble along not too unproductively, approximating in our work when it is dependent upon sampling; discussing the issues when our tests are described and pursuing contextual variables through analysis of trait-treatment interaction. But there are deeper problems than these. First, measures of gross yield as criteria for standard procedures cannot be acceptable in relation to education. Second, meaningful action is not quantifiable and distributed systematically and cannot be controlled or sampled.

Let us consider each of these in turn.

Measures of gross yield are acceptable as criteria for selecting a standardized procedure only on the assumption that the procedure cannot appropriately be varied within the population, and this assumption is not acceptable in education. The problem can be translated into agricultural terms. A measure of gross yield is an appropriate basis on which to select a crop treatment in large-scale farming, where a standardized procedure in which some plants do not thrive is more acceptable than a diagnostic cultivation of each plant individually. In education, however, it is possible to vary procedures rather than to standardize them. The teacher is like a gardener who treats different plants differently and not like a large-scale farmer who administers standardized treatments to as-near-as-possible standardized plants. Under such conditions variation of treatment gives a better gross yield attempting to maximise the yield of every individual unit; and this is what is required in education. The teacher must diagnose before he prescribes and then vary the prescription. The agricultural model assumes the same prescription for all.

Thus Cronbach (1975) on Rivlin (1973):

> Some social scientists nowadays are eager to establish rigorous generalizations about social policy by conducting experiments in the field. We have already seen mammoth federal experiments on performance contracting in education, on alternative rules for making 'negative income tax' payments, and on alternative practices in compensatory education. As these experiments have moved towards completion, their advocates have become increasingly pensive. Alice Rivlin, a leader among those advocates, has just reiterated her belief that formal social experiments are worth their cost. But she also (Rivlin, 1973) entertains the thought that their proper use is to compare alternative rules, rules so formal that the winning competitor can be embodied in an act of Congress and enforced uniformly over the nation. The welfare alternatives are of this sort. Rivlin doubts that gross experimental comparison can produce useful rules for schooling, where a treatment is multifaceted, cannot be standardized, and interacts with pupil background. Under these circumstances, the between-school variation in practices swamps out any generalized effect of the specified treatment variable.

Even here there is a nostalgia for the discarded model in the last two sentences, for it is assumed that the impediment to 'rules for schooling' is swamping out of generalized effects of the specified treatment. I argue that we cannot assume any specified treatment is there unless we can accurately detect its generalized effects.

This is because both teachers and pupils are involved in meaningful action and meaningful action cannot be standardized by control or sampled.

Meaningful action is action whose definition cannot be inferred from observed behaviour without interpretation of the meanings ascribed in the situation by participants. Such 'actions' cannot be controlled because meanings cannot be controlled. They cannot be sampled except as 'behaviours' which are then treated as if they were attributes of populations, a simplification which, though it falsifies, is appropriate for actuarial purposes. Both the action of teachers and the (re)action of pupils and contextual actors (parents, principals, other teachers) are meaningful actions of this sort.

Moreover, the assumption is that the meaningful actions in which the teacher is involved *qua* teacher are responsible professional actions for which he is accountable. Given that by participating in educational settings he is in a position to interpret meanings in action, he is not able to fulfil his professional role on the basis of probabilistic generalizations but on the contrary is expected to exercise his judgement in situational analysis. Such situational analysis can draw on intuitive organization of experience, and probabilistic generalizations, and theory. The maximum contribution from the last two of these is desirable.

Probabilistic generalizations are of the actuarial kind which assure bookmakers of their winnings and make gambling with them a gamble. Teachers are in the position of gamblers rather than book-makers because they are dealing with individual situations, not large populations of situations. But they are able to make diagnostic moves in order to verify generalizations in cases. This requires an attitude of systematic enquiry which is like research except that it is not normally presented publicly.

Much more significant than probabilistic generalizations about the effects to be expected from procedures is theory, because theory supports the interpretation of the meaning of situations. Theory is not predictive: predictions have to be derived from it by interpreting the theory into the situation in which the prediction is made. Theory can also be used to read rapidly the significance of the unpredicted.

There is a modestly developed theory of the context and conditions of educational action available in psychology and sociology. But there is little theory of educational action itself; and this would be the heartland of a theory of education. Such theory would also be necessarily testable by the teacher (and by other educational practitioners) since action theory is clearly testable by action research. (Action research is here construed as research in which an experimental procedure must be justified as an act in a substantive field of action – here education – rather than purely in research terms.)

The development of a theory of education is impeded by the pursuit of probabilistic generalizations linking procedures to output criteria. Such a research strategy is atheoretical and delegates to the teacher the theoretical task of interpretation. But it is the researcher who should take a leadership role in creating such theory in collaboration with teachers. To offer correlations and statistical predictions to teachers who need causes is to make the assumption that the teacher is a better theorist and presumably a better tester of theory than the professional researcher.

Perhaps it is difficult for the researcher to admit practitioner research because it means a diminution of his power *vis-à-vis* teachers. Unless he is a good theorist, he may become merely a technical consultant. For beyond that his position depends upon his ability to make better meanings from data to which teachers have equal access than the meanings the teachers themselves can make. The laboratory experiment offers more prospect of this than does the psycho-statistical experiment. But the laboratory will have to look very like a classroom, and the experimenter very like a teacher.

References

CAMPBELL, D.T. and STANLEY, J.C. (1963) 'Experimental and quasi-experimental designs for research on teaching' in N.L. Gage (ed.) *A Handbook of Research on Teaching* Chicago: Rand McNally.

CRONBACH, L.J. (1975) Beyond the two disciplines of scientific psychology *American Psychologist* 30, 116–27.

FISHER, R.A. (1935) *The Design of Experiments* Edinburgh: Oliver & Boyd.

RIVLIN, A.M. (1973) Social experiments: the promise and the problem *Brookings Bulletin* 10, 6–9.

SNOW, R.E. (1974) Representative and quasi-representative designs for research on teaching *Review of Educational Research* 44, 265–91.

WALKER, D.F. and SCHAFFARZICK, J. (1974) Comparing curricula *Review of Educational Research* 44, 83–111.

The psycho-statistical paradigm and its limitations 2*

I would go so far as to doubt whether most of the work in psychology and sociology which is taught to prospective teachers has any close relevance to educational practice. Its relevance is to educational theory, that is, to a kind of theory which is to be tested by educational practice. The error is to attempt to apply results to educational practice rather than to use educational practice to test results. And the error is made by the researchers in the first instance. They appear to claim that their research does not ask for verification in educational practice.

However, there has been a research tradition which has paid much closer attention to problems of educational practice than those traditions at which I have glanced so far. Dominant in this research on teaching, which is largely concerned with curriculum, classroom process and teaching methods, is the so-called 'psycho-statistical paradigm' (Fienberg, 1977). This research paradigm originates in agriculture and its prophetic book is Ronald Fisher's *The Design of Experiments* (1935). (I am personally indebted to my former colleague, David Hamilton, who pointed out to me how illuminating it could be to return to this source.)

The paradigm is familiar to all of us here, I assume. The major breakthrough is the insight that random sampling is to be preferred to sampling judged to be representative because randomization allows the use of the mathematics of probability to estimate error, and to develop tests of significance. The structural threats to validity are comparability of the experimental and the control samples, known as the problem of internal validity, and comparability of both samples with a target population to which generalizations are to be made, known as the problem of external validity.

In agricultural research block and plot designs are used to randomize

* From 'Applying research to education', unpublished paper, mimeo, 1978.

soil and aspect or other similar conditions; non-experimental variables such as, for example, fertilizer, are controlled as is the experimental variable. (Incidentally, a Norfolk turkey farmer, working this kind of design in computerized experiments on factory farming, tells me that he can get experimental effects in a block and plot shed of turkeys which turn out not to hold when replicated in an ordinary open shed.)

In applying this research design to agricultural practice the objective is to make a preferential discrimination between one practical course of action and another. It is important to grasp that a similar design can be used to serve theory by providing a comparative discrimination between theories. The statistics may be seen as a decision-making technique which can be used to make decisions between theories or between practices. In agricultural research and in educational research the application to practice is more often direct than through theory. In education the design is used to attempt to discriminate between curricular specifications or between methods or between teaching styles, for example.

However, the yield of educational experiments which are cast in this mould is increasingly recognized as disappointing. I shall not trouble you with references. Rueful reflections abound. Most often experiments fail to yield statistically significant results. But when they do, there is still dispute on technical grounds. It is impossible to draw random samples in field settings in education. Criteria of yield cannot be established as they can in agriculture.

Campbell and Stanley (1963) have looked at problems of sampling in particular relation to internal validity. Snow (1974) has subsequently reviewed them in relation to external validity. Both are cautiously optimistic. Walker and Schaffarzick (1974) are more pessimistic about criteria, at least in the area of curriculum, finding from a broad review of American work that curricula show up well when tested by instruments which favour them. Cronbach (1975), who has been hot on the heels of trait-treatment interactions, is now intensely sceptical, and even calls for humanistic approaches.

In this country the disillusionment has been less explicit, but the reaction towards more descriptive, less statistical approaches is here represented as what has come to be called 'the illuminative approach'. Is the dominant paradigm in research in teaching proving ineffectual? I think it undoubtedly is. But why?

I want to argue that it is not because of technical shortcomings in sampling and statistical procedures that the classic designs are failing us. It is because of a misplaced conceptualization of the application of research to education.

First, let me assert the principle of individualization of treatment in education. I can illustrate this by comparing agriculture with careful gardening. In agriculture the equation of invested input against gross yield is all: it does not matter if individual plants fail to thrive or die so long as the cost of saving them is greater than the cost of losing them. If it costs X + Y to hoe a field and the loss from not hoeing it is crop yield worth only X, then you don't hoe. This does not apply to the careful gardener whose labour is not costed, but a labour of love. He wants each of his plants to thrive, and he can treat each one individually. Indeed he can grow a hundred different plants in his garden and differentiate his treatment of each, pruning his roses, but not his sweet peas. Gardening rather than agriculture is the analogy for education.

Now, assuming a perfectly executed experiment in teaching – the perfect sample, the perfect criterion measure – we should be able to conclude that if a teacher is compelled to adopt a single uniform procedure for all cases, he is better to adopt X than Y. However, that condition is an important one: the discrimination of the relative effectiveness of two alternative procedures by the use of an experiment cast in the psycho-statistical paradigm is an effective guide to action only if a standard procedure must be used in all cases. At system level this implies uniformity of treatment in all schools irrespective of context. At classroom level this implies uniformity of treatment of all children.

Now there are many, I imagine, who, like myself, regard teaching as an art in which the teacher's skills are differentially applied as a result of diagnostic interpretation. Teaching is largely a response to the observation and monitoring of learning in cases. If this is so, then a crucial problem of the psycho-statistical paradigm as the design for a discriminant experiment is not simply that it deals in general prescriptions, but that it offers to guide teachers by overriding, rather than by strengthening, their judgement.

In essence the design offers a measure of the probability that one procedure uniformly applied is superior by some criterion to an alternative procedure uniformly applied; it deals in terms of odds, and suggests where one might place one's bet. But it does little or nothing to explain differences of outcome between procedures.

Of this design I have said elsewhere:

. . . without understanding *why* one course of action is better than another, we could prove by statistical treatment that it is. The vision is an enticing one: it suggests that we may make wise judgements without understanding what we are doing and the difficulty of understanding what we are doing had been thought to be the barrier to wise action. (Stenhouse, 1978)

I could elaborate at a length quite inappropriate to this occasion a critique of evaluation of educational procedures by the use of the psycho-statistical model, and for today I must ask you to accept that such an elaboration would be reasonably coherent, if contentious. It involves the rejection of behavioural objectives as alternatives to hypotheses, the preference of norm-referenced over criterion-referenced tests (which are types of examination rather than research instruments), and the rejection of random sampling in research into areas of action. It argues that the breakdown of sampling necessitates a return to the study of cases. But it does not involve a rejection of quantitative approaches, of measurement or of statistical operations; some statistical techniques, such as time-series analysis, are obviously relevant to the study of cases. Moreover, I believe sampling can be rethought. Of course, I do not claim to have done all this work. I am arguing for a shift of paradigm on the part of at least a proportion of researchers, for testing a new approach.

The key to this approach is the application of research to education through an appeal to teacher judgement. The assertion is that the improvement of teaching rests upon the development of the art of the teacher and not through the teacher's adoption of uniform procedures selected from competing alternatives.

If this is the way ahead, then we need a theory of teaching, and experimental results which do not make a theoretical contribution are little worth. I am, of course, only echoing B.O. Smith (1961) and Ian Westbury (1971) among others; I think I am extending the area of research in which the claim is being made, for I see tremendous theoretical potential in experimental action research based upon curriculum and teaching strategies, where their reference was mainly to observational research.

The point of view I am taking implies that research is best applied to education by producing theory which can enrich action. The action is the action of the teacher, and this implies that the theory of teaching must be understood by the teacher. Of course, this calls for greater research literacy among teachers, but it also calls for much more accessible research and theory. Since I believe that most educational theory is made more inaccessible to practitioners than it need be – not only because we researchers have a tendency to self-display, but also because we have personal intellectual needs which cannot entirely be sublimated into chess and crosswords – I think theory would actually be improved by being made more accessible.

Above all, however, a theory of educational action must be recognized as hypothetical. That is, its status as knowledge is provisional and subject to revision. Moreover, its defects may be limitations of generalization so that it serves as a framework within which theories of individual cases have to be developed. Such a theory cannot prescribe action, but can support only the development of experimental actions which test and refine or elaborate the theory. In short, an empirically-grounded theory of educational action will require continuous revision and development through experiment, and much of that experiment will not be large-scale field experiment, but rather laboratory experiment.

There is thus a need for the development of educational laboratories. In them we shall have to control conditions so that we can simulate faithfully those of real classrooms . . ..

But wait a minute! That would seem to imply that wherever there is a real classroom there is a potential educational laboratory. Just so. The best designed educational laboratories are in charge of teachers, not of researchers.

The function of educational research in its application to practice is to provide a theory of educational practice testable by the experiments of teachers in classrooms. In a sense this calls for the development of the role of teacher as researcher, but only in a minimal sense. The basic desideratum is systematic enquiry; it is not necessary that this enquiry be made public unless it offers a contribution to a public theory of education.

Such a view of educational research demands of teachers the capacity to see educational action as hypothetical and experimental. Researchers on this view should disseminate to teachers a scepticism about research results and theories and hence a disposition to test them. Research should underwrite speculation and undermine assertion.

Research can be adequately applied to education only when it develops theory which can be tested by teachers in classrooms. Research guides action by generating action research (or at least the adoption of action as a systematic mode of enquiry). Action research in education rests upon the designing of procedures in schools which meet both action criteria and research criteria, that is, experiments which can be justified both on the grounds of what they teach teachers and researchers and on the grounds of what they teach pupils. A systematic structure of such procedures I call a hypothetical curriculum. Such a curriculum is the appropriate experimental procedure through which research is applied by testing, refining, and generating theory in the laboratory of the classroom.

References

CAMPBELL, D.T and STANLEY, J.C. (1963) 'Experimental and quasi-experimental designs for research on teaching' in N.L. Gage (ed.) *A Handbook of Research on Teaching*, Chicago: Rand McNally.

CRONBACH, L.J. (1975) Beyond the two disciplines of scientific psychology *American Psychologist* 30, 2, 116–27.

FIENBERG, S.E. (1977) Next steps in qualitative data collection *Anthropology and Education Quarterly* 8, 2, 50–7.

FISHER, R.A. (1935) *The Design of Experiments* Edinburgh: Oliver & Boyd.

SMITH, B.O. (1961) 'A concept of teaching' in B.O. Smith and R.R. Emmis (eds) *Language and Concepts in Education* Chicago: Rand McNally.

SNOW, R.E. (1974) Representative and quasi-representative designs for research on teaching *Review of Educational Research* 44, 3, 265–91.

STENHOUSE, L. (1978) Case study and case records: towards a contemporary history of education *British Educational Research Journal* 4, 2, 21–39.

WALKER, D.F. and SCHAFFARZICK, J. (1974) Comparing curricula *Review of Educational Research* 44, 1, 83–111.

WESTBURY, I. (1971) 'Problems and prospects' in I. Westbury and A.A. Bellack (eds) *Research into Classroom Processes* New York: Teachers College Press.

The illuminative research tradition*

We may sum up the situation by saying that work in the psycho-statistical paradigm offers to do better than professional judgement in judging what best to do, and that in overriding professional judgement it fails to strengthen it. It appeals to research judgement: if the design and conduct of my research is correct, then my results must be correct. If you think they are wrong, then fault the design and conduct *of the research*.

The important point about the illuminative tradition is that it broke away from this and aimed to appeal to, and hence to strengthen, professional judgement. The aim in the end is professional growth in educators: teachers, advisers, administrators. From this desire to appeal to professional judgement comes a range of concerns about presentation and about audiences. In particular, there is a need to capture in the presentation of the research the texture of reality which makes judgement possible for an audience. This cannot be achieved in the reduced, attenuated accounts of events which support quantification. The contrast is between the breakdown of questionnaire responses of 472 married women respondents who have had affairs with men other than their husbands and the novel, *Madame Bovary*. The novel relies heavily on that appeal to judgement which is appraisal of credibility in the light of the reader's experience. You cannot base much appeal to judgement on the statistics of survey; the portrayal relies almost entirely upon appeal to judgement.

The commitment of the illuminative tradition to appeal to judgement has meant that it cannot create samples by abstracting features from cases. Such abstraction is fundamental to the psycho-statistical experiment.

Illuminative research has thus been associated with the study of cases, not of samples. Much of this work is communicated in words,

* From The problem of standards in illuminative research *Scottish Educational Review* 11, 1, 1979.

but there is a lot of room in case study for a quantitative ingredient which is at present too much neglected. We need to ask what dossier of statistics one would gather to place a school within the range of schools: site value; library borrowings; number of visitors, and so forth. Also, the potential of such techniques as time-series analysis needs to be explored. The issue is not qualitative versus quantitative, but samples versus cases, and results versus judgements.

Experimental design and research in classrooms – an example*

Our job in the project team was to design a research from which they (i.e. the teachers) and we learned as much as possible from their educational actions. This meant that we had to respond to educational actions in a spirit of systematic enquiry. Working in this way, primarily in research terms, is a characteristic of action research. We had to work alongside teachers, respecting their educational aims and professional judgement, but trying ourselves to learn as much as we could for a wider audience about the 'Problems and Effects of Teaching about Race Relations'. We wanted to ensure that the participating teachers had the best possible opportunity of learning too. Both their needs and our own meant that it was part of our job to support them as they developed a research role alongside their main role of teaching.

How does one design a research to capture educational acts in a spirit of enquiry? One way is to attempt to cast them in the form of an experiment: another is to observe them carefully and record them. An experiment is shaped to sharpen the bearing of observations on certain questions, and if possible to enable observation to be expressed as measurement. Naturalistic observation responds to the natural shape of events and attempts to portray them in a way that makes them open to people who did not have first-hand experience of them. We tackled our problem from both ends, using both experiment and descriptive case studies. In experiment we are fishing for generalizations; in case study we are portraying experiences that while they do not offer general laws, can be applied to the new situations we meet as all thought-through experience can.

We shall look first at the problem of experimental design in our action research context.

Let us begin by bringing to mind a pattern of classical experimental

* From *Teaching about Race Relations: Problems and Effects* (with G. K. Verma, R. D. Wild, and J. Nixon) Routledge & Kegan Paul, 1982.

work in the psychological laboratory. A group of people is divided into two apparently comparable groups, called an 'experimental group' and a 'control group'. The experimental group is given some treatment whose effects interest us and the control group is not. The control group might be called a 'comparison group'. The performance or condition of the two groups is measured or observed before the experimental treatment is given to the experimental group and then again after the treatment. Any difference that is observable in the two groups after the experiment but not before is taken to be the result of the experimental treatment. This design can be expressed thus:

Time

Experimental group	O X O
Control group	O O

Where O = observation or measurement and X = experimental treatment.

This sounds very simple, but there are a number of problems that must be overcome if reasonable conclusions are to be drawn from such an experiment. For example, the experimental and control groups must be comparable with each other; the experimental treatment must be consistent throughout the experimental group; the measuring instrument must be consistent for both groups; the control group must not be exposed to any chance treatment relevant to performance on the measures; and no contextual conditons likely to affect the observed performances of the groups must bear on them during the experiment. These conditons are difficult to meet, but unless we succeed in meeting them the results we are comparing inside our experiment will not really be comparable.

The problem of the comparability of experimental and control groups concerns our ability to make statements about the effect of an experiment. We compare an observation or a measurement result in a group where we have mounted an experiment with one in a group where we have not, and attribute any difference to the experimental treatment. For example, we might compare the effects of a new reading programme in schools. If we did so, it would be important that the two groups taking the programmes were comparable in all the variables relating to performance in reading. This problem of comparability within the experiment is crucial to our making valid statements about what has happened in the groups we have observed.

It is an aspect of the problem of internal validity.

Internal validity can best be ensured by conducting the experiment 'under laboratory conditions'. This is because a laboratory is designed to enable us to control the variables that may, if uncontrolled, destroy comparability.

However, a laboratory is a privileged place in this respect, and often the effects we get there do not generalize reliably to real settings. Unless we are testing a theory, which brings together a lot of differing observations and makes sense of them, we shall usually find it difficult to generalize the effects observed within a laboratory experiment to the rough-and-ready conditons of real life. The laboratory is useful (and currently too neglected) in educational research, but it is for clarifying and refining theory. This is because it is difficult to generalize the results of the laboratory experiment by predicting the results to be expected outside the experiment, in a target population that concerns us in the real world. The problem of generalization to situations outside an experiment is that of external validity.

One could tackle this problem by making the laboratory more and more like the world outside. Educational laboratories might simulate real classrooms.

This observation makes it obvious that an alternative procedure is to conduct experiments outside the laboratory altogther and in real classrooms. Even then, if we have experimented in a limited number of classrooms, we must ask: is what we have discovered applicable to other classrooms in other schools? For example, all the schools except one in the present project are state comprehensive or secondary modern schools; so we would apparently be on thin ice if we attempted to predict from our results what might happen in teaching about race relations in public schools. Thus, the problem of external validity is raised even in classroom-based experiments. Such experiments may be called field experiments; and in their classic form in agriculture they were literally that: fields, such as most readers will have seen, where one fertilizer or strain of seed is tried out against another to see which is best.

The theory behind field experiment is that we can represent the contextual variables by sampling in such a way that they 'cancel out' into a blurred background against which we can get our experimental observation into focus. We want a sample of people and institutions and environments that is representative of the target population to which we want to generalize, or in which teachers want to apply, our results. We want our experimental schools to tell us about other schools out there in the system.

In order to create such a representative sample, however, we should have to know already the distribution of all the relevant contextual variables in the target population and to build them in the same proportions into our sample population. This is an impossible condition to meet. Therefore researchers generally try instead to draw random samples, that is, samples constructed on the principles of chance. The definition of a random sample is: a sample so selected from a larger population that each unit in the larger population has an equal and independent possibility of being selected.

Now, the main argument for random sampling is this. No properly representative sample can be drawn, but so long as the sample is drawn by chance rather than by judgement, it is possible to use the mathematics of probability to assess the chances of a difference observed between an experimental and a control group being due to differences between the samples rather than between results of experimental treatments.

We can observe a difference and calculate, for example, that there is only one chance in twenty of its being an artefact of sampling error (0.05 level of significance), or that the chance is merely one in a hundred (0.01 level of significance). Such calculations of significance are computed in our experiment, but in the last analysis they are weakened as we depart from random sampling, as we always do in field research in education. This is partly because we cannot control schools and teachers and pupils, and hence cannot select them randomly and then ask some to follow our experimental procedure and others not.

We necessarily work with 'opportunity samples', which are 'naturally assembled collectives such as classrooms, as similar as availability permits' (Campbell and Stanley, 1963: 217). Having lost randomization, we need to consider very carefully the sample that opportunity has made available to us.

Our design is apparently one of experimental and control groups using opportunity samples. Within this limitation on sampling, we appear to be concerned with internal and external validity. But what is the experiment about?

The conventional expectation is that it is to test which of three ways of teaching about race relations is best. This is emphatically not what we are attempting to do. Walker and Schaffarzick (1974: 109), surveying all the American studies they could find that attempted to compare curricula in these terms, conclude:

> The difficulties we experienced in trying to interpret the results of these studies led us to question the wisdom of designing and conducting comparative experimental studies of different curricula. Studies which locate the distinctive outcomes of different curricula and studies which determine the long-term school-related and life consequences of these

different outcomes would seem to be more useful both to policy-makers and scholars. Such studies require that a great deal more research be directed towards creating measures of a variety of outcomes other than achievement that commonly appear in claims made for and about curricula.

We agree with this view, the more so because we are concerned primarily with teachers as an audience and only secondarily with policy-makers and scholars. We do not think we have got as far along the road that Walker and Schaffarzick point out as we might have done. This is partly because we have had to address some rather general questions.

The first of these is: does teaching about race relations tend to make the overall situation with regard to interracial attitudes worse rather than better? This is an important question, and one on which opinion has been divided. Stemming from it is another question: are there some particular ways of teaching about race relations that are liable to do damage? Of course, we can face this question only within the context of the teaching styles mounted in this project; and even then it is a difficult one.

We also hoped to pick up from the experiment some indication of trends of attitude among adolescents and to look for consistencies of result that might lead us towards theory; but these matters will be discussed later.

One theoretical line we might have hoped to pursue was closed to us by the constraints of action research. It would have been of great interest to compare the results of a non-authoritarian approach like that of the Humanities Curriculum Project with an authoritarian approach to teaching about race relations. Of particular interest would have been the relationship of these approaches to the reactions of pupils who differ in their attitudes towards school and teachers. However, in the experiment (see page 42), our Strategy B teachers did not in effect take an authoritarian stance, and this possibility was consequently lost to us, since it would have been quite improper for us to attempt to persuade teachers to adopt an authoritarian stance against their better judgement.

The adoption of respect for professional judgement in the classrooms as an ethical basis for the research also prevented us from pressing our teachers to conform to rigid specifications of teaching, and hence the experimental treatments were not tightly controlled.

The limitations we have described are pretty well universal in field experiment in education. Such limitations suggest that we should be wary of over confidence in the validity of predictive generalizations drawn from our sample and purporting to apply to other schools and other classrooms.

So many variables, including some within the control of the teacher, are at work in teaching situations that it seems impossible to tease them out statistically in a way that has meaning for action (Cronbach, 1975). And quite clearly, in respect to teaching about race relations, different factors are at work in, say, a multi-ethnic school in urban Birmingham and an ethnically homogeneous school in Lincolnshire. Inferences drawn from the study of a sample can be applied only precariously in the school system as a whole.

Snow (1974) offers a useful lead here when he points out that, though a sample may not be representative of a prespecified target population, a careful analysis of the sample itself may provide a good judgement of the target population to which it could generalize. He is still thinking in the classic terms of generalization. His point is even more striking if we cast the problem in terms of application of the research to a specific case: that is to say, one's own.

Such an application may be an inference from a sample to one's own case or from another case to one's own case.

Whenever a uniform policy or practice has to be executed throughout a population – of schools, classes or pupils – this shift from generalization to application will be seen as a weakening of the relevance of research to practice. However, in England at least, the general assumption is that schools should adapt to their own situations by differentiating their practice. This is particularly true of a problem like teaching about race relations, where the context and conditions of the teaching vary significantly. In such situations, and given such assumptions, generalizations that are merely couched in terms of probability will always be less favoured than applications based on informed professional judgement. That is why our research is primarily aimed at informing – and, in the longer run, strengthening – the professional judgement of teachers.

We hope to provide the information that will allow a teacher to judge whether his situation would fall within a target population represented by the situations sampled in the research. But we also want to put him in a position to judge that some particular situations within the sample cast light on his own, either because of a similarity or because of a contrast which clearly defines features of the teacher's own case.

This illumination of one's own circumstances by access to the experience of others depends upon the possiblility of recognizing similarities and differences between other cases and one's own. Such recognition depends upon the existence of portrayals of experience, and this is the role of descriptive case studies in the present project.

Our measurement results document some problems of teaching

about race relations, but they tend in their nature to provide data about effects. The title of our project, 'Problems and Effects of Teaching about Race Relations', expresses our belief, formed on carefully assessed experience in two other projects, that the documentation of the problems encountered by good teachers is a better basis for improving one's own practice than the documentation of best practice. Imitation is not the road to better teaching.

The principles underlying the three strategies are principles of navigation, not courses to be followed. We must, as Walker and Schaffarzick (1974: 109) suggest, escape from the literal root meaning of 'curriculum'; must 'stop thinking of the curriculum as a fixed race course and begin to think of it as a tool, apparently a powerful one, for stimulating and directing the active learning capacities which are ultimately responsible for the achievement we want from schools'.

References

CAMPBELL, D.T. and STANLEY, J.C. (1963) 'Experimental and quasi-experimental designs for research on teaching' in N.L. Gage (ed.) *A Handbook of Research on Teaching* Chicago: Rand McNally.

CRONBACH, L.J. (1975) Beyond the two disciplines of scientific psychology *American Psychologist* 30, 116–27.

SNOW, R.E. (1974) Representative and quasi-representative designs for research on teaching *Review of Educational Research* 44, 3, 265–91.

WALKER, D.F. and SCHAFFARZICK, J. (1974) Comparing curricula *Review of Educational Research* 44, 1, 83–111.

WHAT RESEARCH CAN OFFER TEACHERS

Reporting research to teachers: the appeal to professional judgement*

1

I want to make it quite clear that in reporting research I am hoping to persuade you to review your experience critically and then test the research against your critical assessment of your own experience. I am not seeking to claim that research should override your judgement: it should supplement it and enrich it. All too often educational research is presented as if its results could only be criticized technically and by other researchers. But I am arguing that it should be subject to critical appraisal by those who have educational rather than research experience and who are prepared to consider it thoughtfully in the light of their experience.

And thoughful consideration is what I am asking of you. I return to my earlier thoughts about my relation as a reseacher to this audience. You might be tempted to appeal to research as a source of authority which will exempt you from the need to make judgements. You would be making an error if you were to regard this research – indeed, most educational research – in that light.

2

I'm going to ask you to perform sleights of mind which may not come easily to people who know something about measurement. I'd like to ask your first of all to try to forget everything you were taught about

---

* 1 From 'Cultures, attitudes and education': a paper given to the Commonwealth Section of the Royal Society of Arts, and printed in the *Royal Society of Arts Journal* 126, 5268, 1978.

 2 From 'The measurement results: teaching about race relations – problems and effects': a talk given at a DES conference, July 1976. An edited transcript is reproduced in J. Ruddock, *Dissemination of Action Research: Case Record 3* (unpublished).

measurement, in psychology and education, and to assume the position that any results that I present to you are less reliable than your own experience, properly examined. That because those results are in terms of general trends and possibilities, they are not reliable for your own experience, so they have to be tested by your judgement. I'm trying to contrast that with what many people were taught in college – that measurement results could be used to override your judgement – which is a common point of view . . . and I'm trying to say that I think measurement should be subordinate to judgement. If after comparing the measurement results with your own experience you find yourself uncertain of judgement, then basicallly there's no alternative to doing your own research in your own classroom, devising ways of scrutinizing the effects of your teaching. The second thing is that I would like you to assume that the results are intended to contribute to your perception of the situation; they are not intended to discriminate one course of action which would be better for you than another. If the results make a difference to your perception of the situation, they make a difference to your planning of action in the light of that perception.

What I am trying to do is to encourage the feeling that all the statistics can be thrown out if they don't accord with the reality as you know it, and when you look at statistical results, somehow the thing to do is to end up not talking about standard deviations but talking about experience.

How teachers can use research – an example*

My concern as a teacher is whether to teach about race relations in social studies and, if so, what approach to use. Let us say that my problem is, more particularly, that I teach social studies in the form of a human issues programme covering such topics as the family, poverty, people and work, law and order, war and society, relations between the sexes, and I wonder whether to include race relations. A complicating factor is that my style of teaching controversial issues is to set up among adolescent students discussions of such evidence as, for example, newspapers, stories, pamphlets, photographs and films; and to act as neutral chairman in such discussions, the better to encourage critical attitudes without taking sides. In short, I have been influenced by and am in the tradition of the English Humanities Curriculum Project (1970, 1973).

I am very concerned that my teaching should contribute positively to race relations in my multi-racial society if that is possible. I wonder whether I should teach about race relations at all. If so, I wonder whether it is appropriate in this case to take the role of neutral chairman, even though this is a teaching convention and not a position professing personal neutrality. So I turn to a research report on 'Problems and Effects of Teaching about Race Relations' for enlightenment.

Here I find that the project has monitored on a pre-test, post-test basis two different strategies of teaching about race relations, one in which the teacher is neutral (called Strategy A), the other in which the teacher feels free to express, whenever he feels it appropriate, his committed stance against racism (called Strategy B). Strategy A was conducted in fourteen schools and Strategy B in sixteen schools. The samples are not true random samples because of problems of accessibility of schools and students, but I know something about this from

* From 'Using research means doing research' in H. Dahl, A. Lysne and P. Rand (eds) *Spotlight on Educational Problems* Festskrift for Johannes Sandven, Oslo University Press, 1979.

my study of education at college (Campbell and Stanley, 1963; Bracht and Glass, 1968; Snow, 1974).

Control groups have been gathered in the same schools as the experimental groups whenever this was possible, though this was not possible in all cases. I came across this table of results on a scale purporting to measure general racism.

Table 1 Scores on the general Racism Scale of the Bagley-Verma Test. Decrease in score represents decrease in racism.

Teaching Style	Experimental Sample			Control Sample			Significance of difference ** .01 * .05 and t value for difference of difference Experimental and control
	Pre-test Mean & (S.D.)	Post-test Mean& (S.D.)	Direction of Shift & t value for difference of means	Pre-test Mean & (S.D.)	Post-test Mean & (S.D.)	Direction of Shift & t value for difference of means	
Exp. N: 258 Strategy A Control N: 124	17.24 (10.05)	16.51 (10.25)	1.71	16.06 (9.66)	17.61 (10.49)	2.11*	2.83**
Exp. N: 359 Strategy B Control N: 180	17.25 (9.61)	16.17 (9.78)	2.27	17.42 (9.93)	17.87 (10.58)	0.72	1.91

This seems to help me a good deal at first sight. My neutral strategy is Strategy A. Attitudes in the Strategy A Group seem to improve and, though the improvement does not quite reach even .05 level of significance, the control groups, left to general influences, deteriorate in attitude significantly and the comparison of experimental and control shows at least by one criterion a .01 level discrimination in favour of teaching about race relations by Strategy A. Strategy B does not look markedly superior to Strategy A so I don't seem to need to change my teaching style. So it seems that research has helped me by enabling me to decide the right style in which to teach about race relations.

But, oh dear, here's a problem. On a later page the same data are presented in a different form to show the situation in individual schools and this seems to complicated the issue. Here is the table.

Table 2 Differences between pre-test and post-test school means for experimental and control groups on the general racism, anti-Asian and anti-black scales of the Bagley-Verma Test: Strategy A.

1 School Code	2 Experimental GR	3 Experimental AA	4 Experimental AB	5 Control GR	6 Control AA	7 Control AB	8 Comment Code
03	−1.83	−.35	−1.22	—	—	—	C
07**	1.58	.54	.31	−.86	.21	−.71	G
09	−.22	.55	−.9	2.11	1.45	1.09	A
10*	−.63	−.18	−1.54	—	—	—	C
13	−.85	.37	−1.29	−.89	−.56	−.67	D
17	−2.5	−1.17	−1.78	—	—	—	C
18	1.7	2.4	.9	6.63	4.38	3.75	B
19	.37	−.04	.62	—	—	—	D
29	−3.42	−1.75	−1.67	2.0	.87	−.25	A
31**	−.12	.77	.65	.34	.5	−1.16	D
32**	−1.61	−.7	−.83	−.07	−.77	−.38	A
39*	1.2	−.5	1.05	—	—	—	D
Mean of Strategy A controls (individuals)				(1.3)	(.83)	(.49)	

** over 25% non-white

 * 5–25% non-white

Now, looking at this table I personally feel that, given comment codes A, B or C I certainly ought to proceed, given comment codes D and possibly E I should proceed with great care, and given codes F and G, I might be better to give a lot more thought to the matter. In seven out of twelve schools the result seems encouraging; in four schools results seem doubtful and in one rather alarming. How do I know what category my school will fall into? This is really rather disturbing to my decision. Perhaps I should shift to Strategy B. Let's look at the Strategy B table.

Table 3 Differences between pre-test and post-test school means for experimental and control groups on the general racism, anti-Asian and anti-black scales of the Bagley-Verma Test: Strategy B.

1 School Code	2 Experi- mental GR	3 Experi- mental AA	4 Experi- mental AB	5 Control GR	6 Control AA	7 Control AB	8 Comment Code
01	–3.51	–1.6	–2.57	–1.75	1.43	–1.34	A
02	0	–.67	–.10	2.43	1.22	1.43	A
04*	1.04	.10	.24	—	—	—	E
05	–2.27	–.34	–.97	—	—	—	C
06*	–2.00	1.29	–1.30	.55	.34	–.52	D
08	1.09	.30	.07	–5.4	–1.2	–2.33	G
09	–2.89	–.22	–1.97	2.11	1.45	1.09	A
11	–1.58	–.48	–.53	—	—	—	C
14**	–.33	.39	.91	—	—	—	D
15	–2.25	.17	–1.42	—	—	—	C
20	–.39	.05	–.22	–1.15	.86	–1.43	F
21	–1.77	–1.32	–1.19	1.59	1.04	.59	A
24*	.19	.37	.60	4.93	1.07	1.65	B
30*	3.79	1.27	2.16	—	—	—	E
33	1.00	.43	.38	–.83	.83	–.08	G
Mean of Strategy B controls (individuals)				.90	.71	.30	

** over 25% non-white

 * 5–25% non-white

Oh dear! This is no better. Here eight out of fifteen schools are reassuring, three are doubtful and three are alarming. Strategy B seems no refuge.

Can it be that statistically significant discriminations between two treatments when presented through means and standard deviations can mask such a range of within-sample variance as this? It can indeed. In the psycho-statistical research paradigm the effects are not 'other things being equal', they are 'by and large' or 'for the most part'. So doing one thing is only sometimes better than doing the other! Depending on your school context or school environment or perhaps yourself or your pupils, apparently.

What I have to find out now is whether teaching about race relations by Strategy A is good for *my* school. However, that reminds me that I haven't looked at pupils as individuals, only as means and standard deviations. Suppose I took these data and looked at them in a way that depicted the fate of individuals. How about a histogram of change scores? There are of course problems with such scores (Linn, 1974), but, bearing them in mind, I'll give it a go.

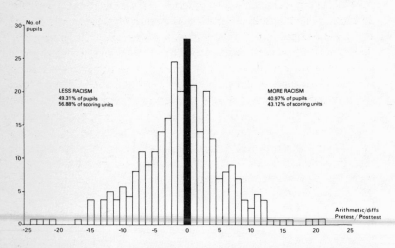

Fig. 1 Histogram of differences between pre-test and post-test scores on general racism scale of Bagley-Verma Test: Strategy A Experimental. (N = 288)

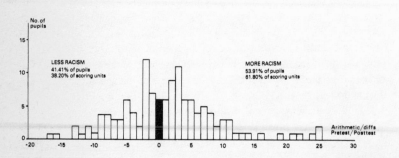

Fig. 2 Histogram of differences between pre-test and post-test scores on general racism scale of Bagley-Verma Test: Strategy A Control. (N = 128)

My goodness, it looks as if the same teaching style and the same subject matter make some people worse as they make other people better. One man's meat is another man's poison. If I teach about race relations, some people get worse. But, then if I refuse to teach about race relations, even more people get worse. I suppose I should have thought of that anyway. I know that when I teach about literature some people come not to like it, but I believe that even fewer would come to enjoy literature if I didn't introduce them to it at all.

It looks as if all schools should not do the same thing. Should I teach material about race relations whether my class is racially mixed or not? I need to steady myself. After all, engineers don't always build exactly the same bridge. Nor do chess players always play the same game. There must be ways of fitting action to situation and perhaps even to individuals in that situation. I've clearly got to think things out for myself. Does this mean that research cannot help me? What was that piece in the paper by Cronbach they gave us in Ed. Psych? Here are my notes. And here it is: 'When we give proper weight to local conditions, any generalization is a working hypothesis, not a conclusion' (Cronbach 1975: 125). That seems to mean that the results of research need testing in local conditions. What research gives me is most often not findings about all teaching but hypotheses about my teaching.

This is a bit of a shock, but it makes reasonable enough sense. And the hypotheses I've got are already of some use. I must test whether Strategy A works well for me in my classroom, whether I can sustain its logic in practice, and whether it is giving good results in attitudes. At the same time I know that even in a good result some individuals will be deteriorating in attitude.

What I am going to do is this. I'm getting a student to come in and pre-test and post-test my pupils and a control group in my school. But I'm also going to tape our sessions on race relations on a portable cassette recorder. To do this I have to tape other lessons too, so that I don't seem to be concentrating on race. I've started this. I'm explaining to the students that I'm doing a study of my own teaching and that this should help me to teach better. And I'm beginning to get them talking about how well my teaching and their learning goes.

Of course, there's a problem about how to handle the tapes. I played some at home and tried a Flanders Interaction Analysis (Flanders, 1970) on them. It did tell me that I talked too much, but not a lot more. Then I tried the Humanities Project analysis which worked quite well because I was involved in discussion teaching. But I want to look at pupil behaviour as well as teacher behaviour. I'm beginning to ask myself whether I can develop a theory of individuals who cause me concern in class. I don't even need paper to do that. I can play cassettes in my car as I drive to and from work. . . .

At the end of this session I'm going to try to set up a club in the district for teacher-researchers. They have clubs for people who tinker with motor cycles to get more performance from them: why not the same for teachers who are tinkering with their teaching?

I'd like to set about testing Piaget. Most of his experiments are a kind of teaching. And I have a feeling that if I work with a small sample, like him, I'll find out quite a lot for myself. I've got a better laboratory than he had: it's a real classroom!

I'm not sure if I'm doing research. I am testing hypotheses by experiment as systematically as a busy job allows.

The Shorter Oxford English Dictionary says that research is: 'Investigation, enquiry into things. Also, habitude of carrying out such investigation.' Well, it is beginning to become a habit.

References

BRACHT, G.H. and GLASS, G.V. (1968) The external validity of comparative experiments in education and the social sciences *American Educational Research Journal* 5, 437–74.

CAMPBELL, D.T. and STANLEY, J.C. (1963) 'Experimental and quasi-experimental designs for research on teaching' in N.L. Gage (ed.) *Handbook of Research on Teaching*. Chicago: Rand McNally.

CRONBACH, L.J. (1975) Beyond the two disciplines of scientific psychology *American Psychologist* 30, 116–27.

FLANDERS, N.A. (1970) *Analysing Teaching Behaviour* Reading, Mass: Addison-Wesley.

HUMANITIES CURRICULUM PROJECT (1970) *The Humanities Project: an Introduction* London: Heinemann Educational Books. Revised by J. Rudduck (1983) and published by the School of Education, University of East Anglia.

LINN, R.L. (1974) 'Change measurement' in S.B. Anderson, S. Ball and R.T. Murphy *et al.* (1974) *Encyclopedia of Educational Evaluation* San Francisco: Jossey-Bass.

SNOW, R.E. (1974) Representative and quasi-representative designs for research on teaching *Review of Educational Research* 44, 3, 265–91.

STENHOUSE, L. (1973) 'The Humanities Curriculum Project'. in H.J. Butcher and H.B. Pont (eds) *Educational Research in Britain 3*: University of London Press.

STENHOUSE, L. (1977) *Problems and Effects of Teaching about Race Relations*. A report to the Social Science Research Council on Project HR 2000/1. (Lodged in the British Library.)

WALKER, D.F. and SCHAFFARZICK, J. (1974) Comparing curricula *Review of Educational Research* 44, 1, 83–111.

How research can contribute to the improvement of teaching*

Research cannot improve teaching without helping the teacher to develop skills in a context of judgement. How can research strengthen the judgement of teachers? Certainly only by appealing to teacher judgement. Such a view of the relationship of research to the improvement of teaching has implications for the development of new styles of research.

Cronbach (1975: 126), schooled in the classic research paradigm, observes that though the researcher 'may reach an actuarial generalization of some power, this will rarely be a basis for direct control of any single operation'. In short, generalizations couched in terms of probability do not *apply* to situations. 'When we give proper weight to local conditions,' says Cronbach, 'any generalization is a working hypothesis, not a conclusion'. Thus, what the classic research procedure offers to teachers is not conclusions to accept but hypotheses that need testing.

This implies that the hypotheses which are the products of research need, if they are to improve the practice of teaching, to be couched in such terms as make them amenable to testing in the classroom. If we ask the teacher to pose the question 'Does this more or less widespread observation hold for my particular situation?' we must in our presentation of the observation give him the means to answer the question we have recommended to him. It is one of the great – but often unexploited – strengths of Piaget's work that, since most of his experiments are cast in the form of teaching or assessment, his work is readily verifiable in the classroom.

There is a sense in which hypotheses emerging from experiments in the psycho-statistical mode must be testable by curricular action if

* From 'Can research improve teaching?': paper given at the Scottish National Conference on Curriculum and Evaluation for PE Teachers, January 1979; printed in *Report: National In-Service Course on Curriculum Design, Course Structure and Evaluation in Physical Education*, Dunfermline College of Physical Education, 1979.

applied by the teacher. A curricular action is one justifiable not only in experimental or research terms but also in educational terms.

But there is a need to supplement experimental styles of research which are sensitive to the needs of application to practice by observational and descriptive styles of research which tutor judgement by extending experience. Here history is the model. It reviews and orders past experience – that of yesterday as well as that of former centuries – and attempts retrospective generalization.

This summary ordering of experience depends upon judgemental rather than mathematical calculation and consequently it demands data accessible to thoughtful consideration. This calls for the realistic portrayal of cases rather than the abstract representation of samples. Cases cumulate, as for example in history we cumulate cases of long-barrow burials or cathedrals or joint-stock companies, but the retrospective generalizations derived from surveying the cumulated cases do not provide predictive generalizations in the classic form: they define rather a gradient of expectation and explore the logic of rarities, seeking to explain what gives rise to the unusual. Retrospective generalization, like the study of individual cases, can improve practice only through an application of judgement to the case in question. In short, the capacity of research to improve teaching depends upon – and in turn feeds and strengthens – the teacher's professional judgement.

A direct way of stating this would be to say that the application of case-study research requires a comparative study of your own case. You must weigh up your own situation against the accounts of other situations.

I conclude that research can only markedly improve the art of teaching if it:

1 offers hypotheses (i.e. tentative conclusions) whose application can be verified because they can be tested in the classroom by the teacher

   or

2 offers descriptions of cases or retrospective generalizations about cases sufficiently rich in detail to provide a comparative context in which to judge better one's own case.

I also believe that at the moment the improvement of schooling depends more than anything else on the development of the art of teaching.

It is clear that if the teacher is to experiment in the laboratory of his own classroom and study carefully his own case he will have to be given more time for planning and reflection. The great barrier to the improvement of teaching is the inexorable load on the teacher's attention of the burden of present contact hours.

Reference

CRONBACH, L.J. (1975) Beyond the two disciplines of scientific psychology *American Psychologist* 30, 2, 116–27.

The case-study tradition and how case studies apply to practice*

Case-study research is to be distinguished from research conducted in samples. Sample-based research is concerned to establish by calculation the relationship between a sample studied and a target population to which the findings in the sample are to be generalized. This enables variables in the sample to be abstracted from context. Context, seen as an impediment to generalization, is not required as a basis for making judgements about the representativeness of the sample nor does generalization depend upon contextual analysis.

In case study the relationship between a case, or a collection of cases that may superficially resemble a sample, and any population in which similar meanings or relationships may apply, is essentially a matter of judgement. Such judgement depends heavily upon assessments of multivariate complexes and of contexts, and it consequently demands a degree of descriptive verisimilitude or close interpretation of cases. Abstraction starves judgement of this kind.

Judgements of cases cumulate into prudence: 'the ability to discern the most suitable, politic, or profitable course of action; practical wisdom, discretion.' (Oxford English Dictionary). As Habermas (1974: 44) remarks: 'On the road toward science, social philosophy has lost what politics formerly was capable of providing as prudence.' Case study reaches after the restoration of prudence – and also of perceptiveness: the capacity to interpret situations rapidly and at depth and to revise interpretations in the light of experience.

Indeed, the case-study tradition may be seen as a systematization of experience within which interpretations are critically handled in the interests of preventing experience from becoming opinionated.

There are two major traditions of case study on which educational work may be seen to be drawing: the historical and the ethnographic.

* From 'A note on case study and educational practice': a paper given at a conference at Whitelands College, London, July 1982, and published in R.G. Burgess (ed.) *Field Methods in the Study of Education*, Falmer Press, 1984.

The relationship between the two is complex and I cannot even attempt to unravel it here. However, some points are worth making as placing controversy on profitable lines.

First, history is essentially documentary, concerned with the discussion and interpretation of evidence accessible to scholars. Ethnography, though it draws on field notes, seldom treats them as documents to be made available for critical discussion, depending for confirmatory responses upon the reader's experience of like situations, the cogency of the theory offered, and perhaps trust in the ethnographer.

Second, there is a sense in which history is the work of insiders, ethnography of outsiders. In its origins history has been how the ruling classes write about their own society; ethnography has been how they write about the societies of others. As these traditions have developed, history has been addressed to knowledgeable audiences – the history of trades unions to trades unionists, of horticulture to horticulturalists – and has relied on the knowingness of the reader. The historian, assuming a shared understanding of human behaviour, deals in the foreground of action. The ethnographer, by contrast, has used a degree of naïveté as a tool to call into question the commonplace. Originally concerned with exotic cultures, ethnography has become a means first, of studying exotic elements within our own culture, later, of rendering the familiar exotic, a device whose capacity to illuminate was demonstrated fictionally by *Gulliver's Travels*. Ethnography calls the cultures it studies into question rather than building on their taken-for-grantedness. Lévi-Strauss (1968) expressed this by suggesting that historical explanation is in terms of the conscious, while the explanations of social anthropology are in terms of the unconscious.

What both history and anthropology have in common is that they deal with events and situations embedded in time: they are both concerned with the past and any timelessness they may achieve is a transcendence of this. Further, both offer thick descriptions: that is, representations whose virtue is verisimilitude as opposed to abstracted analyses.

How do they apply to practice?

First, descriptive case studies of any kind provide documentary reference for the discussion of practice: workshop materials for practitioner groups. This is a simple, but an important, function. When practitioners – or others – discuss problems of educational practice, they each commonly refer to a unique personal experience. It is as if each calls up private pictures of schools without realizing the extent to which this divergence of reference disables discussion.

Personal experience needs to be referred to tabled cases in order to make it publicly available. Case studies are important as evidence.

Second, and only slightly less direct, is the relevance to practice of the comparison and contrast of other cases with one's own case: the case which above all one must come to understand if one's practice is to be effective. Whether the other cases be historical or ethnographic, such comparisons tend to open up new perspectives on one's own case, generating both a consciousness of one's knowingness and a sense of the accepted as problematic. One might see the most developed product of such comparison as an interpretation or a theory of one's own case.

Third, crucial to practice is critique, that is to say, a systematic body of critical standards by which to interpret and evaluate practice. An excellent example of such critique in action is the informed discussion of such a sporting event as a cricket match in which the interpretation and evaluation of the play rests on the discussants' experience of many cases of such matches. The improvement of critique of classrooms and schools is central to the problem of quality in education, and it depends heavily upon practitioners extending vicariously their experience of schools and classrooms as cases.

Fourth, the setting of such a critique within a broader social and political analysis (critical theory?) depends by definition on the development of the critique that is to be so disciplined by contextualization.

Finally, there is the question of theory that could be tested, or at least applied, at the level of rather general principles. Most social science and most history falters here in respect of education. Social science too often produces concepts (jargon) that seem stepping stones into a lake rather than across a river. History loses its grasp of the concrete (which is its strength) and falls back upon abstracted forces or trends which can too readily be preserved by ingenious interpretaion. Case study seems to have been weak here, but then research which promises to produce stronger theory also seems to have failed. Perhaps general theory at the level of cause and effect is scarcely appropriate to educational study. Certainly, if it is appropriate, then it will have to stand the test of the study of cases: probabilistic theory exempted from the need to apply in every case is of little interest in such practical affairs as the practitioner is concerned with.

There will, of course, be some who think that I am demanding too rigorous a style of theory: to my mind, rigour is the *sine qua non* of theory. Where we cannot achieve it, then we are better to follow interpretative and humanistic traditions (fashionably dubbed 'hermeneutic') than to use scientific paradigms.

Two final points. In an interpretative tradition, wise saws and aphorisms have their place: 'Schools that set out to change society will discover new ways of conserving it'; 'Open access to office holders and democracy are contradictory principles in schools: access makes sense only when it is access to power'. And, second, a pedagogy may be an acceptable alternative to theory. Such a pedagogy would suggest patterns of classroom action that enable the pursuit of educational aims to be a means of capturing an understanding of educational process. In short, the possibility of studying one's case as one lives it may be built upon our case-study tradition to the extent that the objectives of education and of the study of education can be fused in action.

References

HABERMAS, J. (1974) *Theory and Practice* Heinemann Educational Books.
LÉVI-STRAUSS, C. (1968) 'Introduction: history and anthropology' in C. Lévi-Strauss, *Structural Anthropology* Penguin.

Action research and the teacher's responsibility for the educational process*

1

This week I want to introduce the idea of action research. It is a difficult idea to introduce because *action research* is defined and used differently by different individuals in different contexts. The two papers I have given you in support of this evening's work, that by Robert Rapoport and that by Nevitt Sanford, make that plain enough, so I'm not going to burden you with sectarian theology. What I want to do is look at the problem of arriving at a general definition of action research and then examine the implications of this definition.

Rapoport starts:

> Action research is a type of applied social research differing from other varieties in the immediacy of the researcher's involvement in the action process. Some social scientists have differentiated action research from the larger field of applied research by the existence of a client with a problem to be solved. The social scientist, in this context, becomes what Bennis calls the 'change agent'.

But Rapoport feels that this is not an adequate definition and he proposes this reformulation: 'Action research aims to contribute *both* to the practical concerns of people in an immediate problematic situation and to the goals of social science by joint collaboration within a mutually acceptable ethical framework.'

This seems a useful reformulation, but I want to push it a little further and apply it to education. For me the helpful distinction is not between social scientists and practitioners but between a research act and a substantive act. A research act is an action to further an enquiry. If you ask someone to explain why he did it, he will answer: to find something

---

* All three extracts are from the transcripts of seminars with the part-time M.A. students at CARE (1979; 1981).

out. A substantive act is justified by some change in the world or other people which is judged to be desirable. In education, substantive acts are – to oversimplify a little – intended to help people to learn.

Consider now the situation of pure research. The research act and the substantive act are hardly at odds. The researcher acts to find out and his substantive task is so to find out that others can verify and use his findings in a research context. Research produces *theory*, the main purpose of which is to summarize what we know in such a way as to guide further research. In Rapoport's terms social science research simply serves 'the goals of social science.'

Action research is the type of research in which the research act is necessarily a substantive act; that is, the act of finding out has to be undertaken with an obligation to benefit others than the research community. This is what we mean when we say that children are not to be used as guinea pigs.

Let me make this clear and concrete. The Humanities Curriculum Project set out to investigate the problems and possiblilities of teaching about controversial human issues, our race project to investigate problems and possibilities of teaching about race relations. The Ford T Project of John Elliott investigated the problems and possibilities of teaching through enquiry and discovery. In order that each of these investigations should proceed, teaching about controversial issues, teaching about race relations and teaching by enquiry and discovery had to take place.

Now, it is the teacher's responsibility to decide and hold himself accountable for the educational process in his classroom. In no circumstances, I claim, can he relinquish this responsibility to a researcher. He cannot properly say that he is teaching HCP because the project team said he should, nor can a project team properly *tell* teachers how they should teach.

Hence in action research the teacher has full and responsible control of the research act while the researcher's responsibility is to ensure that the maximum learning is gained from the teacher's acting as he does – through an act at once an educational act and a research act.

This relationship is the basis for the claim I would make that in action research the researcher should be accountable to the teachers. This does not mean that he should be directed by them what to do, but that he should be required to justify his acts and report to the teachers.

The relationship I have described is threatened by the assumptions of teachers about research and also by the balance of power and status between teachers and researchers in our society and the implications of power at the centre in the so-called centre-periphery model. It has only partly been implemented in all the projects I know of, though progress has been made, and it remains in my view a realistic long-term aspiration.

For me this has a further profound implication. I do not believe that action research in education should contribute, as Rapoport has it, '*both* to the practical concerns of people in an immediate problem situation and to the goals of social science'. I would not as a teacher consent to take part in action research which helped my immediate problems and beyond that simply contributed to social science. I believe that social science makes comparatively little contribution to educational practice, because its theories are oriented towards guiding research rather than towards guiding teaching.

So I would want to ask any action researcher what contribution his work is making to a theory of education and teaching which is accessible to other teachers. I want the audience for action research to be teachers, not social scientists.

Finally, I believe that a theory of education derived from action research should be testable through action research. That is, teachers should, within the limits of their time, be able to test the results of action research by monitoring their own practice, its context and its results. It is the strength of action research in curriculum and teaching that its utilization does not depend upon teachers' accepting its hypotheses, but on their testing them.

2

The essence of action research I think is that one makes a substantive move (by 'substantive' I mean a move that has got meaning and significance in a particular area of action) and that one makes it with the prospect of pupils' learning in mind. You cannot for example set up two parallel groups in your classroom – an experimental group for whom you are trying to do your best and a control group for whom you are trying to do your worst – because you have no right to do your worst. As teachers you are charged with operating for the benefit of the learning of your pupils. Action research in education always implies that at the heart of the research is an action which has to be justified in these terms.

3

When you do action research the crucial thing is tight specification – knowing what you are doing. And knowing what you are doing means writing a curriculum. It means getting absolutely clear what the curriculum you are experimenting with is. Imagine the Brothers Wright and the aeroplane. There was a design – a blueprint or a drawing. In order to do the research you have got to make the aeroplane. It's no good as it were running along the tarmac flapping your arms. You have actually got to create some sort of instrument. And if you are teaching in a spirit of enquiry then the curriculum counts as the specification of the action research. . . . Action research relates to the curriculum in such a way that the curriculum constitutes a definition and specification of the experimental procedure.

References

RAPOPORT, R. (1970) 'Three dilemmas in action research' *Human Relations* 23.
SANFORD, N. (1970) 'Whatever happened to action research?' *Journal of Social Issues* Summer, 26, 3.

Section 2

Curriculum

Within the context of the curriculum, research feeds action and helps teachers to theorize about their teaching. The curriculum is a specification that is hypothetical, open to question and testing, and within which knowledge is constructed and negotiated. By working within a model of curriculum development that specifies principles of procedure rather than one that prescribes behavioural outcomes, professional judgement can be effectively developed: the technological means-ends model tends to devalue the importance of professional development by denying the significance of process. Teaching is more than a technology that can be mastered; it is an art, and the artist is the researcher *par excellence*. Crucial to judgements of quality in the arts is the concept of form. Form is process disciplined by standards. Ideas are tested, in form, through practice, and ideas are adjusted in the light of reflection on performance. Teachers, as artists, must be trusted with the responsibility of professional judgement.

J.R. & D.H.

DEFINING THE CURRICULUM PROBLEM*

On my desk before me is a book of 350 pages. It is called *Mønsterplan for Grunnskolen*. I bought it in a bookshop in Oslo. It is the curriculum of the Norwegian comprehensive school.

Beside it is an Open University coursebook, *Thinking about the Curriculum* (Bell, 1971). On page 9 I read:

> What we shall do here is to offer a definition which can serve temporarily both as a starting-point for our discussion and as a comfort for those who like to have precise statements as a guideline for their thinking. However, as you will find, we qualify this definition constantly as we develop our ideas in the units that follow. It is no 'catch-all' definition by any means, and should never be regarded as such. Here it is: a curriculum is the offering of socially valued knowledge, skills and attitudes made available to students through a variety of arrangements during the time they are at school, college or university.

Is the Mønsterplan a curriculum? Or is the curriculum what happens in Norwegian schools?

If the latter, I shall never know it. I cannot get five years leave of absence to attempt to describe all the diverse things that happen in Norwegian schools. And five years is not enough.

I asked a Norwegian curriculum research worker if the Mønsterplan was followed in the schools. He said that it was widely followed, but that many older teachers resisted it and did not follow it, particularly in methods. There was, however, little reformist departure from it. Only tradition seemed strong enough to resist it. Tradition in a sense kept alive the old curriculum of the unreformed school.

How far does the curriculum tie the teacher down? I asked. If I observe him in the classroom, how much of what I see is determined by the Mønsterplan?

I was told that the teacher always had the Mønsterplan in mind, but that it left him a fair degree of individual freedom. It defined a minimum coverage of subject matter and the outline of a method.

* 'Defining the curriculum problem': paper given in Norway, 1973 and published in the *Cambridge Journal of Education* 5, 2, 1975.

It sounded like a child's colouring book, I thought. . . .

I find the definitions of curriculum I have come across unsatisfactory because the problems of curriculum I have encountered in practice as a curriculum research worker slip through them. Perhaps, then, it would be better to attempt to define 'the curriculum problem'.

The curriculum problem most simply and directly stated is that of relating ideas to realities, the curriculum in the mind or on paper to the curriculum in the classroom.

The curriculum problem lies in the relationship of the Mønsterplan to the practice of the Norwegian school.

Notionally the essence of curriculum might be located in the relation of my own ideas as a teacher to the reality of my classroom: 'the true blueprint is in the minds and hearts of the teachers' (Spears, 1950). But the plural here is important. Except for empirical micro-studies of the classroom, the private curriculum of the individual teacher is not of central interest. What is of practical importance in curriculum work is the public curriculum or curricula, that is, curricula that can be held to be in some sense and to some extent publicly accessible to 'the minds and hearts' of many teachers.

Thus, a curriculum may be said to be an attempt to define the common ground shared by those teachers who follow it. Although it may sometimes be useful to think of it as the offering to pupils, we must always bear in mind that any similarity between the offering in one classroom and another, in one school and another, must begin in the like-mindedness of teachers. Most commonly this like-mindedness is a matter of tradition. Induction into the profession includes induction into the curriculum. The formulation of the curriculum tradition may be partly a matter of paper–syllabuses, even government reports or Handbooks of Suggestions to Teachers, but it is largely an oral process. And it is often largely oblique, the indirect communication of assumptions and premises through discourse which rests on them rather than states them.

This curriculum tradition is potent. Some mastery of it is required of the new teacher before he be accepted as a 'professional'; so the teacher learns to define himself by it. In so far as it is not formally stated, analysed and defended, the traditional curriculum is not easily subjected to criticism. In so far as it is institutionalized in the school system, the school, textbooks and the classroom, the traditional curriculum, however critical I may be of it, is not easy to escape. And as the observation of my Norwegian acquaintance suggests, the traditional curriculum is a force strong enough to resist all the pressures of a centralized educational system where, as is the case in

Norway, policies are based on a remarkable degree of social consensus.

Philosophers are likely to be impatient of the traditional curriculum because it is so badly formulated, and its position is so strong that its adherents can afford to neglect justification of their position. Social reformers who, unable to create a new society through political action, hope to do so through the schools are also impatient of the traditional curriculum. It holds the old order in place.

But it is not necessary to question the school either philosophically or socially to want to change the curriculum. Even in its own terms the traditional curriculum is unsuccessful. The greater part of any population is not in the traditional sense either educated or accomplished.

This is not because teachers and educational administrators are uncommonly stupid or lazy or inefficient. It is just that schools are, like factories or shops or football teams, ordinary and imperfect human institutions. We sometimes appear to forget that this much will always be inevitable. Perhaps the school's commitment to educational ideals and high principles fosters optimism.

Curriculum change is necessary and, if it is of real significance, difficult. It is bound to be partial and piecemeal even in centralized systems where educational edicts by no means always command those to whom they are addressed. It always has to fight the comfort of tradition. 'Habits are comfortable, easy and anxiety-free' (Rubin, 1971). For a teacher, taking up a new curriculum is as difficult as going on to a rigorous diet.

In short, it is difficult to relate new ideas to realities.

The problem is to produce a specification to which teachers can work in the classroom, and thus to provide the basis for a new tradition. That specification needs to catch the implication of ideas for practice.

A curriculum is a specification which can be worked to in practice.

A new curriculum will never be secure until it accumulates around it a tradition. The strain of a uniformly self-conscious and thoughtful approach to curriculum is in the long run intolerable. No doubt self-critical analysis is always desirable, but not analysis of everything. New curricula, too, however much the idealist may regret it, must develop comfortable, easy and anxiety-free habits – though not be captured by them.

A new curriculum expresses ideas in terms of practice, and disciplines practice by ideas. It is, I would maintain, the best way of dealing in educational ideas. In curriculum the educationist's feet are kept on the earth by the continual need to submit his proposals to the critical scrutiny of teachers working with them in practice. And because they are related to practice, ideas become the possession of the teacher.

The ideas of a curriculum must be understood, and understood in their relation to practice. The practice of a curriculum must be subject to review in the light of understanding of ideas, but much of it must be learnable as skills and habits. All action cannot be reflective and deliberate.

If curriculum change depends on the writing of specifications of ideas in terms of practice, how are we to do this? There appear to be some working in the curriculum field who believe we can do this by taking thought. I believe that we can only do so by observing classrooms. If a curriculum specification is to inform practice, it must be founded on practice.

The central problem of curriculum is in curriculum change and consists in the task of relating ideas to practice by producing – in whatever form – a specification which will express an idea or set of ideas in terms of practice with sufficient detail and complexity for the ideas to be submitted to the criticism of practice and modified by practice with due regard to coherence and consistency as well as piecemeal 'effectiveness'.

Such specifications can only be written from the study of classrooms.

It follows that a new curriculum must be implemented in practice before it is defined. A group of people, usually including curriculum workers and teachers, must work together and in dialogue on defined problems and tasks until they begin to develop a new tradition which is a response to those problems and tasks. This tradition must then be translated into a specification which transmits the experience captured by the experimental teachers to their colleagues at large.

Exploration must precede survey, survey must precede charting.

This is the basic justification for curriculum experiment.

References

BELL, R. (1971) *Thinking about the Curriculum* The Curriculum: Context, Design and Development, Unit 1. Bletchley: The Open University Press.

RUBIN, L.J.A. (1971) *A study of Teacher Retraining* Santa Barbara: University of California, Centre of Coordinated Education quoted in B. MacDonald and J. Rudduck, (1971) Curriculum research and development projects: barriers to success *British Journal of Educational Psychology* 41, 2, June, 148–54.

SPEARS, H. (1950) *The High School for Today* New York: American Book Company quoted in E.C. Short and G.D. Marconnit (1968) *Contemporary Thought on Public School Curriculum* Dubuque, Iowa: Wm. C. Brown, 1968.

A VIEW OF CURRICULUM

Building a perspective*

1

My view of curriculum research and development is based on the proposition that all curricula are hypothetical realizations of theses about the nature of knowledge and the nature of teaching and learning. The function of curriculum research and development is to create curricula in which these are made articulate and explicit and thereby subject to evaluation by teachers. Such curricula are media in which ideas are expressed in forms which make them testable by teachers in the laboratories we call classrooms. And my contention would be that when curricula are not articulate and hypothetical but implicit and traditionally sanctioned, then pupils are the subject of uncontrolled and unmonitored experiments. This is the condition of most schooling.

2

A straightforward case is that of *MAN: a Course of Study* which claims to be a translation into educational practice of ideas previously expressed in book form by Jerome Bruner. The curriculum specification in such cases provides a practitioner with a vantage point from which he can handle the critical interaction between educational ideas and educational proposals and the critical interaction between these proposals and day-to-day practice. It is possible that the students as well as the teacher will learn more, simply because of the teacher's intelligent exploration through the curriculum of ideas about teaching and knowledge.

* 1 and 3 are from Product or process? A reply to Brian Crittenden *New Education* 2, 1, 1980.
2 is from 'Evaluating Curriculum Evaluation', in C. Adelman (ed.) *Politics and Ethics of Educational Evaluation*, Croom Helm, 1984.

3

Curricula educate teachers and pupils as plays educate actors and audiences. *Waiting for Godot* invites us to explore the nature of life through the process of theatre and meanwhile develops the art of the actor. *MACOS* invites us to explore the nature of knowledge through the process of education, and meanwhile develops the art of the teacher. For this to work we must see that curricula are hypothetical and always flawed.

What is a curriculum?*

What is a curriculum as we now understand the word? It has changed its meaning as a result of the curriculum movement. It is not a syllabus – a mere list of content to be covered – nor is it even what German speakers would call a *Lehrerplan* – a prescription of aims and methods and content. Nor is it in our understanding a list of objectives.

Let me claim that it is a symbolic or meaningful object, like Shakespeare's first folio, not like a lawnmower; like the pieces and board of chess, not like an apple tree. It has a physical existence but also a meaning incarnate in words or pictures or sound or games or whatever.

In our imagination let us bring it into this room. The doors open and it enters on a porter's barrow, since it is too heavy to carry. Two large boxes are full of books for pupils to use in the classroom. A third contains educational games and simulations and a fourth, posters, slides, filmstrips and overhead projector transparencies. The big box over there is the film set (or is this the video-tape version?) and the smaller one beside it contains audio-tape and gramophone records. The seventh, and in this case the last, box holds the teachers' books and materials.

Who made it? Well, perhaps a curriculum research and development group funded by Nuffield or the Schools Council or the American National Science Foundation or Stiftung Volkswagenwerk. Or perhaps a group of teachers from various parts of the country working under an editor for a publisher. Or perhaps a teachers' centre group. Or a school – Abraham Moss or Stantonbury or some less fabled place.

So there it stands, a palpable educational artefact. But what use is it to a student or a teacher? Often apparently, not much. Like some

* From 'Curriculum research and the art of the teacher': a paper given at the annual conference of the Association for the Study of the Curriculum, Brighton, 1980, and published in *Curriculum* 1, 1, Spring, 1980.

wedding presents it is in a month or two more likely to be found in the attic than in the living room. But that analogy is not quite right. A better one is the affluent outhouse containing the unused golf-clubs, canoe, sailing dinghy, skis, ice skates and glider. All the possessions which implied not simply ownership but learning, the development of new skills, on the part of the owner – Mr Toad's curriculum of derelict skiffs and canary-coloured caravans. Material objects cast aside because the teacher was not prepared to face the role of learner they forced upon him.

'No curriculum development without teacher development', reads one of the poker-work mottoes we hung on our wall during the Humanities Project and haven't taken down. But that does not mean, as it often seems to be interpreted to mean, that we must train teachers in order to produce a world fit for curricula to live in. It means that by virtue of their meaningfulness curricula are not simply instructional means to improve teaching but are expressions of ideas to improve teachers. Of course, they have a day-to-day instructional utility: cathedrals must keep the rain out. But the students benefit from curricula not so much because they change day-to-day instruction as because they improve teachers.

*   *   *   *   *

A curriculum, if it is worthwhile, expresses in the form of teaching materials and criteria for teaching a view of knowledge and a conception of the process of education. It provides a framework in which the teacher can develop new skills and relate them as he does so to conceptions of knowledge and of learning.

*   *   *   *   *

Only in curricular form can ideas be tested by teachers. Curricula are hypothetical procedures testable only in classrooms. All educational ideas must find expression in curricula before we can tell whether they are day-dreams or contributions to practice. Many educational ideas are not found wanting because they cannot be found at all.

If someone comes along asking you to adopt an idea or strive after an objective – political maturity or basic literacy – ask him to go away and come back with a curriculum. Or give you a sabbatical to do so for him. What does 'back to basics' mean? What books? What procedures? What time allocations? What investments?

*   *   *   *   *

The curriculum movement of the 1960s and 1970s has pursued the hypothesis that the improvement of the knowledge content of education can be achieved only by developing the art of the teacher to make possible enquiry-, discovery-, and discussion-based modes of learning. The shift is like the shift from apron stage to proscenium or from realism to the theatre of the absurd. The argument is that pupils need to know earlier what mature experts understand about the speculative function of knowledge.

The barriers to that development, apart from the contextual lack of understanding provided by some local authorities, teacher educators, HMI and the like, are that for the most part neither teachers nor pupils recognize teaching as an art. Hence teachers do not see their own development as key to the situation in the same way as actors or sculptors or musicians do. And pupils do not understand – nor do teachers generally share the understanding with them – the significance of experiment in the classroom and their role in it.

No change can be introduced without being explained and justified to pupils. No experiment can be mounted without its purposes, duration and criteria being presented to pupils and without their being invited to monitor its effects on them, both in process and in outcome.

We must be dedicated to the improvement of schooling. The improvement of schooling is bound to be experimental: it cannot be dogmatic. The experiment depends on the exercise of the art of teaching and improves that art. The substantive content of the arts of teaching and learning is curriculum.

The curriculum as hypothetical*

This paper opposes the managerial view of the curriculum as a specification for controlling and standardizing schooling.

From my point of view as a teacher, a curriculum – that is, a proposal specifying a content/methods bundle as clearly as possible – has the status of a suggestion as to what it might be worthwhile (given certain premises) and feasible (given certain conditions) to teach and learn in my classroom. I may have this proposal made to me and be interested in following it up, or I may propose the curriculum to myself. In either case its worthwhileness in practice and its feasibility in the conditions in which I have to work constitute hypotheses.

In order to test this hypothetical curriculum I shall be advantaged if I can enlist the cooperation of my students: they and I together need to evaluate the hypotheses. This means negotiating the curriculum, its evaluation and its possible modification with them. Such negotiation must take account of constraints: for example, even in democratic States a national or State authority or school board may have legislated or mandated that I teach, the students learn, a defined curriculum. In all cases I am constrained by having to work within the limitations of my own knowledge and skills.

We cannot prove that this year's curriculum will serve appropriately for next year since contextual variables will change. Thus the view put forward here is a view supportive of critical pedagogy as a generally appropriate teaching style rather than as a response to a non-recurrent innovative situation.

How might I negotiate with my students to implement such a pedagogy and put the idea of hypothetical curriculum into action? What are the implications of teaching in a style that generates criticism of, rather than acceptance of, the curriculum? For example,

* 'The curriculum as hypothetical': abstract of a paper that Lawrence Stenhouse was to have given at the 1983 American Educational Research Association Conference.

how do I teach if I wish to teach sceptically, questioning rather than accepting the truth of the history book or the science curriculum that the State has prescribed? Under what conditions might it be safe in terms of student order and political expediency to treat curriculum hypothetically in this way? Is such teaching emancipatory? Is emancipation approved?

Testing curriculum
hypotheses in the classroom*

(**HT** Harry Torrance; **LS** Lawrence Stenhouse)

HT   Implicit in 'education' is the possibility of both initiation and liberation through knowledge. But at present the traditional curriculum message is essentially initiatory: knowledge is a possession of teachers which students must respect while mastering it.

LS   Curricula are media in which statements about the nature of knowledge are enacted as learning and teaching. When the enquiring eye of curriculum research treats these enactments of knowledge as problematic and open to question – not to be made unquestionable by teachers and school boards – it reveals that all classrooms can be seen as laboratories, all teaching as experiment, all children either as guinea pigs or as partners in the curriculum research enterprise.

HT   Curriculum theory as talk about curriculum behind closed doors raises questions about the problems of knowledge out of the earshot of students and teachers. In the world of action which students and teachers inhabit these questions are resolved within an ideology of control, the resolution at the same moment redefining and reproducing that ideology. This takes place in the face of the threat which disorganization presents to teaching and learning. To challenge claims to knowledge is to challenge control. Students and teachers come to be on the receiving end of that-which-is (on the authority of others) -worth-knowing. Currently then the authority of know-

* From 'Curriculum knowledge and action: a dialogue' (with Harry Torrance): paper given at the annual American Educational Research Association Conference, Boston, 1980 (unpublished).

ledge is invoked to justify and maintain control. What are needed are pedagogies in which control is not synonymous with, and dependent on, the possession of reified knowledge.

LS   Curriculum is to be tested by students and teachers, not students and teachers by curriculum. And, when we say this, we are talking not of a 'student-centred' curriculum, but of a 'knowledge-based' curriculum. Not a curriculum of skills and information with the knowledge boiled off. A knowledge-based curriculum teaches the problematic nature of knowledge – including knowledge about teaching – in some honest form accessible to its enactors. The medium is the message. The message is a question.

HT   That question is concerned with how knowledge is produced and valued. Schools often constrain intellectual development and the possibility of free and equal participation in democratic debate by ignoring and hence obscuring the process of knowledge production. Our aspiration is for schooling to facilitate an understanding of knowledge as socially generated. In this context a fruitful move might be to elevate everyday reflection and learning to equal status with the academic. We all know a great deal about the world, about our social world, and a formal opportunity to reflect upon one's own process of coming to know things might offer us a purchase on what authoritative others term 'knowledge'.

LS   The function of curriculum is to give everyday reflection about and learning from practice a form in which to work. What plays are for actors and directors – media through which to learn by their everyday activity about the nature of life and their art – curricula are for students and teachers. They are media through which we learn about both knowledge and pedagogy because they invite teachers and pupils to test ideas about both in practice.

HT   If curriculum calls knowledge and pedagogy into question that message must be quite explicit to students as well as teachers. Students' critical responses, insecurities, uncertainties, are generally defined as 'not knowledge', in the same way as teachers' responses have been in many curriculum development projects. Educational researchers, then, exist to improve education and have responsibilities to produce work. But in this they should be accountable to students and teachers by virtue of their ideas being made available to critique through that same work – curriculum. Similarly teachers occupy the same privileged but responsible position *vis-à-vis* students. An educational idea must be self-consciously speculative in its attempt to introduce subject matter for consideration.

LS Teachers and pupils are in classrooms and hence in possession of the laboratories of educational research. Curriculum is a specification of the experimental procedure of action research in classrooms and schools. The curriculum is a hypothesis or conjecture and its adoption should be a sympathetic attempt to refute it. Teachers and students are the crucial evaluators and, if they can evalutate the ideas carried in the curriculum rather than their curricular embodiment, then they can transcend evaluation and reach research.

A VIEW OF CURRICULUM DESIGN

The objectives model: some limitations*

The basic argument underlying the traditional model of curriculum design is as follows. Education is concerned with producing changes in students' performance or behaviour. This formulation derives from definitions of learning used in psychology; and it reflects the behaviourist standpoint. The next step is to assert that the behaviours we hope to produce can be prespecified. In teaching, it is argued, we should know in rather precise terms what changes in behaviour we are attempting to produce in our students. There is a clear implication both that all students should manifest the same behaviour and that it is relatively easy to predict the behavioural results of teaching.

The process of producing behavioural objectives goes like this. We start with our educational aim, and, if we can think clearly enough, we should be able to list ways in which students' behaviour will change if we achieve that aim. 'The student will be able to . . .' is our opening phrase. We are able to translate our aim into quite precise statements of the changes in behaviour we want to see in students, and we say before we begin to teach what these will be. There is an assumption that, having pre-specified these changes, we shall know how to teach for them.

If possible, we also describe the 'entry behaviours' of students – what they are able to do before the teaching starts. A definition of entry behaviours tells us where we are: a definition of behavioural objectives tells us where we want to be. Then education becomes merely a matter of taking a means to an end (see Tyler, 1949).

The action pattern is as follows:

1 specify behavioural objectives (destination)
2 specify or test entry behaviour (point of departure)

* From 'Teacher development and curriculum design'. A paper given at a curriculum conference, University of Trondheim, Norway, 1975 (unpublished).

3   design curriculum and teach students
4   test whether they have achieved the behavioural objectives.

In practice, entry behaviour is generally monitored by a pre-test, and achievement of behavioural objectives by a post-test, the test in both cases being derived by criterion referencing from the behavioural objectives. There are a number of snags in this procedure which cannot concern us here (see, for example, Stake, 1971; MacDonald-Ross, 1973; Walker and Schaffarzick, 1974; Stenhouse, 1975). We can note that, provided the teacher specifies his objectives, the above model can be worked by psychologists or psychometrists who know very little about the classroom, which is often treated as a 'black box' (with the teacher inside!).

The paradigm makes evaluation apparently quite straightforward, and indeed this ease of evaluation is one of the main attractions of the objectives model. It was shaped by the concerns of examiners rather than of teachers or curriculum developers. The first handbook of the *Taxonomy of Educational Objectives* (Bloom *et al*, 1956) is described as 'by a Committee of College and University Examiners'.

This is not the place to offer a detailed account of the objectives model. Such accounts are readily accessible. But we can review its strengths before we look at its weaknesses. First, as we have said, it fits well with a tradition of educational research founded on psychology because it suggests that, once you define its product in terms of objectives, education can be the subject of experiments similar to those conducted in the improvement of agriculture. Such experiments resemble in design those employed in psychology but they use objectives instead of hypotheses. This can be seen as defining the applied nature of the field. Second, since the objectives model provides simple and straightforward criteria for the success of education – the attainment of objectives – it makes the evaluation of education rather simple. Third, teachers are led to think analytically about what they are trying to achieve when they teach by involvement in the process of formulating or reflecting upon objectives. Other advantages are argued in the literature.

However, there are some marked disadvantages of approaching the problem of curriculum through objectives, and these rest, I think, on the oversimplification involved. Experimental design and evaluation pose subtle problems to which enthusiasts for the objectives approach appear blind. Reflecting on objectives does not greatly help the teachers to achieve them if they are suitably ambitious.

I want here simply to draw attention to four points at which I believe the objectives model to be badly founded.

1   It does not draw on, nor is it in accord with, empirical studies of
    the classroom. Those studies which exist suggest that for the most
    part this is not how students learn nor how teachers teach.
    Teaching and learning at their best unfold, are built up and do not
    aim at a goal: they build as high as they can. To the assertion that
    teachers do not work by aiming at a goal, Popham (1968) rejoins:
    'They ought to.' I think he means that they would teach better if
    they did, but I believe him to be wrong. Experiments with
    payment by results in England and performance contracting in the
    United States, as well as more moderate applications of the
    objectives pattern, suggest that only the weakest teachers will
    teach better. Objectives almost inevitably define a standard for
    what Dahllöf (1971) has called the 'steering group' somewhere
    towards the bottom of the group being taught. For the better
    teachers they lower the level of aspiration.

2   Analysis of curriculum content into behavioural objectives is not
    in accord with the nature and structure of knowledge – with
    epistemology. Knowledge cannot be reduced to behaviours. In
    particular it cannot be expressed in terms of pre-specified
    performances for it is the function of knowledge, as opposed to
    mere agglomerations of facts, that it does not determine behaviour
    but liberates it. Knowledge is a basis for diversity of performances
    characterized by understanding. An approach through objectives
    attempts to standardize behaviours, i.e. make them more the
    subject of formulae, less of creative response. Objectives also tend
    to make knowledge, which is the right end, the means to the
    development of skills, which should be the means but are made
    the end. Because of this failure to face the idea of knowledge as the
    basis of enlightenment and understanding, the approach through
    behavioural objectives tends to trivialize the purposes of
    education.

3   Normally, the objectives formula sidetracks and blurs the ethical
    and political problems associated with the control of education, its
    aspirations and its individualization. Whose objectives are these to
    be: those of the State, of the curriculum developer, of the teacher
    or of the student? Should all students in the same classroom group
    have the same objectives? How should objectives be differen-
    tiated? If there are alternative sets of objectives within the same
    curriculum, how do you examine or evaluate? As it is, our classes
    and teaching vary from year to year and in nominally similar
    classes in any one year. We do not know why. We cannot predict

what we shall achieve. Certainly, in our country, examinations
set lower standards than good teachers hope to achieve because
they set *common* standards for all pupils whereas much of the
highest achievement is highly individual. Because we cannot
predict educational events and effects reliably, public
specifications of objectives in practice set low goals. And too
often the very specification discourages teachers from seeing
how far they can go: it imprisons the pupils within the limits of
our hopes.

4   All this leads me to the assertion that the objectives model
over-estimates our capacity to understand the educational
process. It may increase the *clarity* of our intention but it does
little or nothing to improve its *quality*. Nor does it really increase
our capability of realizing our aspirations, for it does not
adequately face the multi-variate situation of the classroom. In
summary, it is not the best basis for teacher development. You
might say it smartens teachers up a bit, making every day more
like the day the inspector visits the classroom. But we all know
the brisk and tidy deceits put on for the classroom visitor, and I
think we shall find the objectives model has similar effects. The
deft teacher can, if he will, achieve the publicly-appreciated
objectives without undertaking the burden of educating the
pupils! Many teachers working in examination classes achieve
this already. They ensure passes for pupils who do not
understand the subject.

References

BLOOM, B.S. *et al.* (1956) *Taxonomy of Educational Objectives: 1 Cognitive Domain*
Longman.
DAHLLÖF, U. (1971) *Ability Grouping, Content Validity and Curriculum Process
Analysis* New York: Teachers' College Press.
MACDONALD-ROSS, M. (1973) 'Behavioural objectives: a critical review'
Instructional Science 2 Amsterdam: Elsevier.
POPHAM, W.J. (1968) 'Probing the validity of arguments against behavioural goals'. A
symposium presentation at the Annual American Educational Research Association
Meeting, Chicago, 7–10 February 1968; published in R.J. Kibler, L.L. Barker and
D.T. Miles (1970) *Behavioural Objectives and Instruction* Boston: Allyn and Bacon.
STAKE, R. (1971) Testing hazards in performance contracting *Phi Delta Kappan*
June, 583–9.
STENHOUSE, L. (1975) *An Introduction to Curriculum Research and Development*
Heinemann Educational Books.

TYLER, R.W. (1949) *Basic Principles of Curriculum and Instruction* Chicago: University of Chicago Press.

WALKER, D.F. and SCHAFFARZICK, J. (1974) Comparing curricula *Review of Educational Research*, 44, 1, 83–111.

The inappropriateness of the objectives model in some content areas[*]

When the (Humanities) Project was set up (and even now), a particular model for research design in curriculum was dominant. This was an output model, based on objectives.

The procedure suggested was as follows. A general statement of aim should be analysed into objectives – I prefer intended learning outcomes – which should be behavioural in the sense that they specified changes in student behaviour (in the psychological sense of that term) which it was intended that the curriculum should bring about. A curriculum should then be constructed and tested, so far as possible by measuring instruments, for its success in teaching the objectives.

This design was not adopted in the Project.

I have written elsewhere (Stenhouse, 1964, 1968, 1970–1, 1971) of my reservations concerning the objectives model. A detailed discussion would be inappropriate here, but some reservations are worth listing:

1 Objectives tend to be *ad hoc* substitutes for hypotheses. They do not lead to cumulative theory. Hypotheses are therefore generally preferable.
2 The use of objectives assumes a capacity to predict the results of curricula which is not justified by empirical work.
3 Consequently, statements of objectives tend to be oversimplified and self-fulfilling.
4 A centrally-designed curriculum development (project) tested by reference to objectives formulated by the central team in detail must imply teacher-proofing. Our curriculum assumed divergent interpretations of a general aim by teachers.

* From 'The Humanities Curriculum Project', in H.J. Butcher and H.B. Pont (eds), *Educational Research in Britain No. 3* London University Press, 1973; reprinted in L. Stenhouse *Authority, Education and Emancipation* Heinemann Educational Books, 1983.

5 The use of objectives tends to make curriculum instrumental and to distort the intrinsic value of content and process. It leads to the concept of an exercise.

6 There are epistemological objections to the idea that all knowledge and understanding can be expressed in terms of specifiable student behaviours.

7 It may be appropriate for the students following a course to have objectives of their own which are to a certain extent divergent.

8 In an exploratory development which enters little-charted areas, there is a need to approach the problem of effects speculatively, and in particular to aim at generating hypotheses from case studies.

9 A curriculum may have important effects on teachers and on schools as institutions, not simply on student performance.

For these and other reasons we adopted a process rather than an output model. Given an aim couched in terms of knowledge and understanding (and perhaps also advanced and complex skills), it is possible to devise a teaching process and teaching materials which are consistent with that aim. In this case the aim is analysed into learning process or input, rather than into i.l.o.s or output.

This procedure allows a gradual exploration of the logic and structure of a subject area, both during a curriculum project and by teachers developing a project's work. Instead of i.l.o.s the input model deals with effects which are hypothesized from case studies of practical situations. It aims to produce a curricular specification which describes a range of possible learning outcomes and relates them to their causes. The style of its formulation is: 'If you follow these procedures with these materials with this type of pupil, in this school setting, the effects will tend to be X.'

The problem with the input or process model is its complexity. Among its strengths are that it is amenable to the hypothetico-deductive method and hence gives greater promise of a cumulative science of curriculum; it avoids the philosophically dubious position that all knowledge can be expressed as learned behaviours; it allows of students having divergent objectives within the same curriculum; and it attempts to face the complexity of the classroom.

References

STENHOUSE, L. (1964) Aims or standards? *Education for Teaching* 64, 15–21.
STENHOUSE, L. (1968) The Humanities Curriculum Project *Journal of Curriculum Studies* 1, 1, 26–33.

STENHOUSE, L. (1970–1) Some limitations of the use of objectives in curriculum research and planning *Paedagogica Europaea* 6, 73–83.
STENHOUSE, L. (1971) The Humanities Curriculum Project: the rationale *Theory into Practice* 10, 3, 154–62.

The case for a process model of curriculum development 1: knowledge and understanding as significant curricular aims*

I argue that, although education is inevitably concerned with the transmission of skills and information, its heartland is in giving access to knowledge as a medium and discipline of thinking. Skills and information can be readily tested and, if it be desired, specified in terms of behavioural objectives. However, an education which merely gives skills and information is an inferior education as compared to that which inducts students into knowledge. The aim of education which offers access to knowledge can be summed up in the word *understanding*. What constitutes understanding in respect of any type of knowledge is problematic from the viewpoint of epistemology.

Now, understanding is demonstrated by the capacity to perform well according to criteria – selecting information and skills appropriately to one's purpose. It cannot be usefully pre-specified in terms of behavioural outcomes; and consequently it is best assessed by means of essays, organized attempts to express one's understanding of phenomena, experiences or problems. My argument is that the assessment of performance in knowledge calls for the specification of the performance which is to be the subject of judgement.

Crittenden (1979) writes:

> Stenhouse seems willing to talk about aims of education, but does not recognize that they cannot effectively guide the process of education unless they are related to learning outcomes through which they are progressively achieved. He refers to the pedagogical aim of the Humanities Project as being 'to develop understanding of social situations and human acts and of the controversial value issues which they raise.' (*sic*) He correctly points out that such understanding can always be deepened (i.e. it cannot be achieved once and for all) and that the criteria of valid understanding are disputed. However, if the aim of understanding in the Humanities Project is to be pursued intelligibly the teacher must at least have some notion of what

* From Product or process? A reply to Brian Crittenden *New Education* 2, 1, 1980.

constitutes an improvement in understanding, and how to recognize it when it occurs. (p. 39)

Quite! Pages 33–36 of the Humanities Project Handbook, which deal with judgement of students' work, meet these points exactly. For example:

> At the same time it is essential to know what counts as success in work aimed at understanding. We therefore offer in this section suggested criteria by which students' work might be judged. These criteria are intended to be principles of judgement for the teacher: the student may well produce work which will stand judgement by these standards without being able to enunciate them.
>
> Teachers will be concerned with judging students' work for two reasons. Sometimes the judgement, whether it be of discussion or of other work, will be part of the diagnostic and self-evaluative process by which the teacher meets his duty to assure himself that individual students or groups are making progress in understanding. In another context, students' performance may need to be assessed and expressed in terms of grades or some other system of public evaluation. (*The Humanities Project: an Introduction* p. 33)

There follow ten suggested criteria for the assessment of work directed towards the aim of understanding.

The implication is that an understanding is a personal achievement in the presence of public criteria. The choice of the word understanding as an aim is illuminated by a consideration of its two opposites, not understanding and misunderstanding. There is an implication of a claim to understand made by an individual who has a subjective experience of closure, an Aha! feeling, but at the same time knows that there exist criteria by which to judge whether his understanding is defensible, whether it is a misunderstanding.

Now, my contention is that while Tylerian objectives work well enough when skills and information are at stake – so far as assessment is concerned – they do not work in respect of knowledge, which is the heartland of the school curriculum. Although knowledge is inferred from behaviours, we cannot pre-specify which behaviours we hope to evince. 'Critical thinking' (cited by Crittenden), even when associated, as Tyler would have us associate it, with a content area, remains a broad aim and not an objective. Its development cannot be held to be sequential in any sense that helps curriculum planning. Nor can it appropriately be tested by any means other than an essay – an original compositon in words or music or visual form – which liberates the learner from the intentions of his teacher. For the essence of knowledge is that it provides standards by which to judge the quality of the unpredicted; it inheres not in behaviours but in the criteria by which behaviour is controlled and judged.

Knowledge cannot be reduced to behaviours. As a medium of thinking its characteristic is that it is supportive of creative thinking and thus indeterminate of behaviours. Pre-specified behavioural objectives necessarily falsify the nature of knowledge. But the falsification is in the pre-specification implied in the term objective. It does not imply that knowledge is not an outcome of education. Indeed, I am arguing that we can judge outcomes without anticipating them. Standards in education, and in curriculum planning, do not depend upon a pre-specification of behavioural outcomes, at any rate in areas of knowledge.

I have made as clear as I can within the confines of this brief outline my conception of the educational process as one governed by standards or criteria which depend upon the judgement of the teacher and my contention that the judgement of the teacher cannot be guided in areas of knowledge by a pre-specification of outcomes. Whence can one derive standards for the selection of content and the criticism of performance? Only, I argue, from the teacher's grasp of the nature and standards of the knowledge being taught. That is why teachers learn subjects.

When I argue for the statement of the curriculum in terms of content rather than objectives, I am suggesting that much should be left to the responsive process of teaching. I wonder how Crittenden teaches. Either he breaks his subject up into a specification of multiple behavioural objectives (which research tells us he should give out to his students) or he accepts a brief specification of content from a university calendar of courses and colours in that outline himself. And no doubt he will teach differently each year, though the calendar is not revised. I think this is entirely proper, and it's certainly what I do myself. Each year the course changes. Each student gets a chance too to follow his bent in his work.

And now I think we are coming to the heart of the matter. I believe that the objectives model actually rests on an acceptance of the school teacher as a kind of intellectual navvy. An objectives-based curriculum is like a site plan simplified so that people know exactly where to dig their trenches without having to know why.

In any knowledge area – say history – begin your curriculum planning by getting a group of colleagues together who are going to teach the subject. Let each define his substantive interest: eighteenth-century diplomatic history, or the history of the Australian rules game (see Hexter's *History Primer*) or the history of banking or the steam engine. Let all agree to read regularly for a year in the philosophy of history and historiography, and then for a second year in classics or historical writing, and during that time to produce some work of his or her own in the chosen substantive area of interest. Relate this to teaching by accepting the curriculum and teaching you are now engaged in as a starting-point. Regularly review examples of pupils' work alongside your own. Are they making the same sort of progress as the teacher group is? Keep tinkering about with the curriculum and the teaching strategies to extract more performance.

If you need more structure, take on a curriculum project in history and use it as a line of development, feeding back evaluative assessment from your classroom and your teacher seminar group and digesting the project until it disintegrates as it is digested to form muscle in your teaching.

References

CRITTENDEN, B. (1979) Product or process in curriculum? *New Education* 1, 2, 35–51.

HEXTER, J. (1972) *The History Primer* Allen Lane: The Penguin Press.

HUMANITIES CURRICULUM PROJECT (1970) *The Humanities Project: an Introduction* Heinemann Educational Books.

The case for a process model of curriculum development 2: respect for forms of knowledge and principles of procedure*

First I must ask, can there be principles for the selection of content other than the principle that it should contribute to the achievement of an objective? There seems no doubt that there can. Peters (1966) argues cogently for the intrinsic justification of content. He starts from the position that education 'implies the transmission of what is worthwhile to those who become committed to it' and that it 'must involve knowledge and understanding and some kind of cognitive perspective, which are not inert' (p. 45). Believing that education involves taking part in worthwhile activities, Peters argues that such activities have their own built-in standards of excellence, and thus 'can be appraised because of the standards immanent in them rather than because of what they lead on to' (p. 155). They can be argued to be worthwhile in themselves rather than as means towards objectives.

In Peters's view the most important examples of activities of this kind are the arts and the forms of knowledge.

> Curriculum activities . . . such as science, history, literary appreciation, and poetry are 'serious' in that they illuminate other areas of life and contribute much to the quality of living. They have, secondly, a wide-ranging cognitive content which distinguishes them from games. Skills, for instance, do not have a wide-ranging cognitive content. There is very little to know about riding bicycles, swimming, or golf. It is largely a matter of 'knowing how' rather than of 'knowing that', of knack rather than of understanding. Furthermore what there is to know throws very little light on much else. In history, science, or literature, on the other hand, there is an immense amount to know, and if it is properly assimilated, it constantly throws light on, widens, and deepens one's view of countless other things. (Peters 1966: 159)

I have already argued that skills are probably susceptible to

* From *An Introduction to Curriculum Research and Development*, Heinemann Educational Books, 1975.

treatment through the objectives model, which encounters its greatest problems in areas of knowledge. Peters is claiming that these areas of knowledge are essential parts of the curriculum and that they can be justified intrinsically rather than as means to ends. They can be selected as content on grounds other than the scrutiny of their specific outcomes in terms of student behaviours.

Within knowledge and arts areas, it is possible to select content for a curriculum unit without reference to student behaviours or indeed to ends of any kind other than that of representing the form of knowledge in the curriculum. This is because a form of knowledge has structure, and it involves procedures, concepts and criteria. Content can be selected to exemplify the most important precedures, the key concepts and the areas and situations in which the criteria hold.

Now it might be thought that this is to designate procedures, concepts and criteria as objectives to be learned by the students. This strategy could, of course, be followed, but it would, I believe, distort the curriculum. For the key procedures, concepts and criteria in any subject – *cause, form, experiment, tragedy* – are, and are important precisely because they are, problematic within the subject. They are the focus of speculation, not the object of mastery. Educationally, they are also important because they invite understanding at a variety of levels. The infant class considering the origins of a playground fight and the historian considering the origins of the First World War are essentially engaged in the same sort of task. They are attempting to understand by using the concept of causation; and they are attempting to understand both the event and the concept by which they seek to explicate it.

It is the building of curriculum on such structures as procedures, concepts and criteria, which cannot adequately be translated into the performance levels of objectives, that makes possible Bruner's 'courteous translation' of knowledge and allows of learning which challenges all abilities and interests in a diverse group.

Reference

PETERS, R.S. (1966) *Ethics and Education* Allen and Unwin.

The process model in action: the Humanities Curriculum Project*

In the Humanities Curriculum Project we rather boldly sought to work to a process model in an area that did not offer the support of a recognized discipline of knowledge and thus a tradition of principles and standards developed by a community of scholars. We started, as Tyler (1949) said we should not, from the examination of a subject or topic area: human issues of universal concern. We were fortunate in being able to diagnose such issues as controversial in the empirical sense that pupils and parents and teachers were likely to disagree about them. More disputably in this country at that time, we posited that teachers might feel accountable to parents and pupils to the extent that they would not wish to use their position of authority in the classroom to advance their own views knowing that these might well be in conflict with the conscientiously-held views of the home.

This position provided us with the idea that we might explore the possibility of teaching to the criterion of neutrality and of enabling students to recognize that controversial issues could best be understood by accepting and interpreting divergence of perception and position.

The construction of our curriculum was the work of a team of eight people over three years, and there is no adequate way in which I can represent that process in a short talk. Note, however, that precisely those traditional types of specification that Tyler criticizes were used to produce one of the most rigorously-specified patterns of content and teaching and learning and assessment achieved by a curriculum project.

Our specification started in a definition of content and of teacher role – Tyler's forbidden 'activities to be carried out by the teacher'[1] – and, if not a generalized pattern of behaviour, yet a similarly general

* From 'Developing curriculum on the process model': paper given at Sheffield Polytechnic, June 1982 (unpublished).

aim: to develop an understanding of human acts, of social situations and of the controversial value issues they raise.

Of course, a curriculum and teaching strategy cannot be derived from definitions of content and teacher and pupil role and aim alone. Intersecting with these are educational principles or values of a more general sort: a desire that education shall socialize or shall emancipate, a conviction that access to knowledge is central to education, a belief that education entails certain values, a preference for rationality over irrationality, for sensitivity over insensitivity, for integrity of feeling over sentimentality and so forth.

The process model rests on the position that such educational principles together with specification of content and of broad aims can provide a foundation for principles of procedure and criteria of criticism adequate to sustain quality in the educational process without reference to closely specified intended learning outcomes. Accordingly, we can teach intelligently and well in knowledge areas while leaving the effects on students problematic. I do not conceive myself as inventing a newer way of handling curriculum development. Rather I am trying to rescue and preserve by discipline the time-honoured ways of conceiving curriculum that Tyler was throwing out.

In short, we do not need to desert traditional specifications for the objectives model in order to bring clarity and rigour into our teaching. We need rather to seek profounder analyses and greater rigour within traditional approaches.

To summarize: one can, I am arguing, intelligently define curriculum in terms of 'activities to be carried out by the teacher' and in terms of content or subject matter, and in terms of highly generalized 'patterns of behaviour' or at least of 'understanding'. Indeed, in areas of knowledge and understanding this is a much better way to tackle curriculum development than through the analysis of an aim into behavioural objectives or intended learning outcomes.

The means of assessment appropriate to such teaching is holistic rather than analytic, and depends upon judgement rather than upon measurement. Measurement is, of course, more reliable, but it is not valid. There is no escape from judgement.

The basis of the kind of assessment implied is the 'essay' in the fullest sense of that word: the trial piece of art or music, of design technology or ecological analysis. Teachers improve this kind of assessment not by analysing an aim into behavioural objectives, but rather by discussing together work by students so that standards of judgement are being thought through.

Now, of course, the process model calls for knowledgeable teachers with sensitivity, thoughtfulness, professional dedication, whereas the objectives model compromises with teacher weaknesses. What I am at pains to point out is that there is no compelling logic about the objectives model in areas of knowledge and understanding. It is less reasonable, less clear-thinking, less rigorous and less profound than the alternative that derives curriculum from educational principles and a consideration of the nature of the knowledge to which we wish to offer students access.

References

TYLER, R.W. (1949) *Basic Principles of Curriculum and Instruction* Chicago: University of Chicago Press.

[1] The key reference was copied out by Stenhouse and attached to the typescript of the lecture.

"Objectives are sometimes stated as things which the instructor is to do; as for example, to present the theory of evolution, to demonstrate the nature of inductive proof, to present the Romantic poets, to introduce four-part harmony. These statements may indicate what the instructor plans to do; but they are not really statements of educational ends. Since the real purpose of education is not to have the instructor perform certain activities but to bring about significant changes in the students' patterns of behaviour, it becomes important to recognize that any statement of the objectives of the school should be a statement of changes to take place in students. Given such a statement, it is then possible to infer the kinds of activities which the instructor might carry on in an effort to attain the objectives — that is, in an effort to bring about the desired changes in the student. The difficulty of an objective stated in the form of activities to be carried out by the teacher lies in the fact that there is no way of judging whether these activities should really be carried on. They are not the ultimate purpose of the educational programme and are not, therefore, really the objectives. Hence, although objectives are often stated in terms of activities to be carried on by the instructor, this formal statement operates as a kind of circular reasoning which does not provide a satisfactory guide to the further steps of selecting materials and devising teaching procedures for the ~~decision~~ curriculum.

"A second form in which objectives are often stated is in listing topics, concepts, generalisations, or other elements of content that are dealt with in the course or courses.... Objectives stated in the form of topics or generalisations ~~$\neq$~~ or other content elements do indicate the areas of content to be dealt with by the students but they are not satisfactory objectives since they do not specify what the students are expected to do with these elements...."

Tyler, 1949.

A VIEW OF CURRICULUM RESEARCH, THE TEACHER AND THE ART OF TEACHING

Curriculum research and the professional development of teachers*

1

For me this chapter is of central importance. In it I shall try to outline what I believe to be the major implication for the betterment of schools emerging from curriculum research and development. Stated briefly, this is that curriculum research and development ought to belong to the teacher and that there are prospects of making this good in practice. I concede that it will require a generation of work, and if the majority of teachers – rather than only the enthusiastic few – are to possess this field of research, then the teacher's professional self-image and conditons of work will have to change.

Let me review some strands in the argument.

First, I have argued that educational ideas expressed in books are not easily taken into possession by teachers, whereas the expression of ideas as curricular specifications exposes them to testing by teachers and hence establishes an equality of discourse between the proposer and those who assess his proposal. The idea is that of an educational science in which each classroom is a laboratory, each teacher a member of the scientific community. There is, of course, no implication as to the origins of the proposal or hypothesis being tested. The originator may be a classroom teacher, a policy-maker or an educational research worker. The crucial point is that the proposal is not to be regarded as an unqualified recommendation but rather as a provisional specification claiming no more than to be worth putting to the test of practice. Such proposals claim to be intelligent rather than correct.

---

* Both extracts are from *An Introduction to Curriculum Research and Development* Heinemann Educational Books, 1975.

Second, in my definition of the curricular problem in Chapter 1, I have identified a curriculum as a particular form of specification about the practice of teaching and not as a package of materials or a syllabus of ground to be covered. It is a way of translating any educational idea into a hypothesis testable in practice. It invites critical testing rather than acceptance.

Finally, in the previous chapter I have reached towards a research design based upon these ideas, implying that a curriculum is a means of studying the problems and effects of implementing any defined line of teaching. And although, because of my own location in the education industry, I have drawn my example from a national project coordinating and studying the work of many teachers, I believe that a similar design could be adopted by an individual school as part of its development plan. I have argued, however, that the uniqueness of each classroom setting implies that any proposal – even at school level – needs to be tested and verified and adapted by each teacher in his own classroom. The ideal is that the curricular specification should feed a teacher's personal research and development programme through which he is progressively increasing his understanding of his own work and hence bettering his teaching.

To summarize the implications of this position, all well-founded curriculum research and development, whether the work of an individual teacher, of a school, of a group working in a teachers' centre or of a group working within the coordinating framework of a national project, is based on the study of classrooms. It thus rests on the work of teachers.

It is not enough that teachers' work should be studied: they need to study it themselves.

2

Hoyle (1972a) has attempted to catch the implications of curriculum development for teachers in the concept of extended professionalism as opposed to restricted professionalism.

The *restricted professional* can be hypothesized as having these characteristics amongst others:

A high level of classroom competence;
Child-centredness (or sometimes subject-centredness);
A high degree of skill in understanding and handling children;
Derives high satisfaction from personal relationships with pupils;
Evaluates performance in terms of his own perceptions of changes in pupil behaviour and achievement;
Attends short courses of a practical nature.

The *extended professional* has the qualities attributed to the restricted professional but has certain skills, perspectives and involvements in addition. His characteristics include the following:

> Views work in the wider context of school, community and society;
> Participates in a wide range of professional activities, e.g. subject panels, teachers' centres, conferences;
> Has a concern to link theory and practice;
> Has a commitment to some form of curriculum theory and mode of evaluation.

I am sceptical about some of this. Why child-centredness, for example? And surely theories should be the objects of experimental testing, not of commitment? The extended professional appears to fall short of autonomy and this is confirmed elsewhere in Hoyle's (1972b) writing:

> This does not mean that we are underestimating the significance of the teacher in the innovation process. The teacher is important in three respects:
> (a) He can be independently innovative at the classroom level;
> (b) He can act as a 'champion' of an innovation among his colleagues;
> (c) Ultimately, it is the teacher who has to operationalize an innovation at the classroom level.

I don't think this limited role and limited autonomy is a satisfactory basis for educational advance. The critical characteristics of that extended professionalism which is essential for well-founded curriculum research and development seem to me to be:

> The commitment to systematic questioning of one's own teaching as a basis for development;
> The commitment and the skills to study one's own teaching;
> The concern to question and to test theory in practice by the use of those skills.

To these may be added as highly desirable, though perhaps not essential, a readiness to allow other teachers to observe one's work – directly or through recordings – and to discuss it with them on an open and honest basis.

In short, the outstanding characteristic of the extended professional is a capacity for autonomous professional self-development through systematic self-study, through the study of the work of other teachers and through the testing of ideas by classroom research procedures.

References

HOYLE, E. (1972a) 'Creativity in the school': unpublished paper given at OECD Workshop on Creativity of the School at Estoril, Portugal.

HOYLE, E. (1972b) *Facing the Difficulties*. Unit 13, Open University Second Level Course: The Curriculum: Context, Design and Development (*Problems of Curriculum Innovation 1*, Units 13–15.) Bletchley: The Open University Press.

Curriculum as the medium for learning the art of teaching[*]

Now the really important thing about curriculum research is that, in contrast to books about education, it invites the teacher to improve his art by the exercise of his art. Teacher education has too often assumed that reading books is the way a teacher gets access to ideas which can be expressed in his practice. Whether they are philosophical works or accounts of experience – such as A.S. Neill's books on Summerhill for example – books tend to put the teacher in the power of the expert. Who can carry a full teaching load and still keep up with the university education lecturer who specializes in Plato or Dewey or Piaget or the expert prominent enough to be allowed to – and even financed to – visit Summerhill, and Countesthorpe and Stantonbury and Gordonstoun?

On the other hand, traditional educational theory – book learning about education – is something you can be very good at without actually getting to know any teachers. In America your status as a university professor of education is actually higher if you have never taught in schools, even when your fame is based on telling school teachers how you think they should teach. In a Scottish college of education the lecturers in education are traditionally exempted from – and thus barred from – supervising teaching practice in order to ensure that they have sufficient time for study to prevent their standards from falling to those of the English!

I am, however, not arguing that all educational thinkers and doers should be teachers, but that all should pay teachers the respect of translating their ideas into curriculum. And that means enough contact with classroom reality or enough consultancy with teachers to discipline all ideas by the problems of practice. I am claiming that the expression of educational ideas in curricular form provides a medium

[*] From 'Curriculum research and the art of the teacher': paper given at the annual conference of the Association for the Study of the Curriculum, Brighton, and published in *Curriculum* 1, 1, Spring, 1980.

for the development – and if necessary the autonomous self-development – of the teacher as artist.

To say that teaching is an art does not imply that teachers are born, not made. On the contrary artists learn and work extraordinarily hard at it. But they learn through the critical practice of their art.

Idea and action are fused in practice. Self-improvement comes in escaping from the idea that the way to virtuosity is the imitation of others – pastiche – to the realization that it is the fusion of idea and action in one's own performance to the point where each can be 'justified' in the sense that it is fully expressive of the other. So the idea is tuned to the form of the art and the form used to express the idea.

Thus in art ideas are tested in form by practice. Exploration and interpretation lead to revision and adjustment of idea and of practice. If my words are inadequate, look at the sketchbook of a good artist, a play in rehearsal, a jazz quartet working together. That, I am arguing, is what good teaching is like. It is not like routine engineering or routine management.

Note, however, that the process of developing the art of the artist is always associated with change in ideas and practice. An artist becomes stereotyped or derelict when he ceases to develop. There is no mastery, always aspiration. And the aspiration is about ideas – content, as well as about performance – execution of ideas.

Thus the process of developing one's art as a teacher – or the art of teaching, which develops through individual artists – is a dialectic of idea and practice not to be separated from change. May I quote Mao Tse Tung without your generalizing my views about life from my choice of source?

> Whoever wants to know a thing has no way of doing so except by coming into contact with it, that is, by living (practising) in its environment.

and

> If you want to know a certain thing or a certain class of things directly, you must personally participate in the practical struggle to change reality, to change that thing or class of things, for only thus can you come into contact with them as phenomena; only through personal participation in the practical struggle to change reality can you uncover the essence of that thing or class of things and comprehend them.

Certainly, this seems true of art, including the practical art of teaching. Perhaps Mao's deviationism was to transpose 'praxis' as a cornerstone of an epistemology with Germanic roots and render it as an expression of the experience of one to whom politics was in practice an art.

In advancing the view that curriculum constitutes both the medium of education of the pupil and the medium for the teacher's learning of the art of teaching, I am making a claim sufficiently novel for me to feel that an analogy may be helpful; but the analogy must not be taken to be too close. It is a crutch to understanding to be thrown away as soon as possible.

I compare a school to a good repertory theatre. With a manager – the head, a company of actors – the staff, a technical support staff – the librarians, lab. technicians, audio-visual experts, and an audience – the pupils or students. Both theatre and school embody the interaction of different groups of people: artists on the one hand, their public on the other. It is as intelligible for a rep. company to claim to have educated its audience as it is for a school to claim to have educated its pupils.

But note that a good repertory company is also concerned with the development of its actors as artists and of the skills and arts of its technicians too. And the medium of this development is the very same medium as that which entertains – motivates – and educates its audience. It is the curriculum of the theatre: the plays.

The good company chooses plays on several grounds. They must overall appeal to an audience. An empty theatre is not really a theatre at all. They ought to be justifiable as worthwhile. So they will say, 'We . . . did *Confessions of a Window Cleaner* in May: we know it's rubbish, but it allowed us to do *Antony and Cleopatra* to a smaller audience in February.' Importantly, however, they should also develop the actors. 'We chose *Antony and Cleopatra* rather than *Othello* because Larry and Viv were just at the point where those parts would most contribute to their development. And, you know, the audience profits immensely from the development of our art. It is not done at their expense.'

There is yet a deeper level at which the artist learns: he not only learns his art, he also learns through his art. Thus the actor learns about life and people and moral dilemmas through participation in plays. And similarly, I learned through teaching literature and history something of what literature and history have to teach.

Curriculum is the medium through which the teacher can learn his art. Curriculum is the medium through which the teacher can learn knowledge. Curriculum is the medium through which the teacher can learn about the nature of education. Curriculum is the medium through which the teacher can learn about the nature of knowledge. And curriculum is the best medium through which the teacher *qua* teacher can learn about these because it enables him to test ideas by practice and hence to rely on his judgement rather than on the judgement of others.

The relationship of 'form' in teaching to the improvement of teaching*

. . . it is clear that the idea of education is sufficiently ambitious to preclude the possibility of perfect performances. No teaching is good enough: therefore good teaching is teaching towards the improvement of teaching. The implication is that all teaching ought to be seen as experimental.

In the sense that it has a high investment in personal skill in proportion to its investment in knowledge, teaching is an art. A teacher can train himself by practice as a ballet dancer or a poet can. But teaching is a human art, not a medium art: its artefact is not manifest in palpable or visible form.

We can make too much of the distinction between science and art, and I don't want to attempt an analysis of the distinction here. I shall claim that art is experimental like teaching, that one element in the science/art continuum is the extent to which experiment is structured by theory or disciplined by critique, and that teaching lies at a middle point in that continuum. It is, at its best, an improvisation on a form, the form structured by theory and consituting a test of theory, the improvisation disciplined by the actors' critique and in dialectic with public critique.

*   *   *   *   *

I believe that in order for teaching to be held to be problematic, it must be formal; and that improvisation by teachers can only meet criteria of quality if it is improvisation on a form as opposed to an intuitive or child-centred formlessness.

I do not see *formal* and *informal* as distinguishing along the same lines as *traditional* and *progressive*; and I do believe that the formal/informal distinction is the more relevant to the quality of education –

* From Teachers for all seasons *British Journal of Teacher Education*, 3, 3, 1977.

so long as the form is held to be problematic.

Let me characterize informal teaching. Informal teaching is based on the assumption that the personal qualities of the teacher, the sorts of things that the teacher believes, the knowledge at the teacher's disposal and the passion with which that knowledge is lived are the most important determinants of the quality of teaching. Teachers are born, not made; and intuition, sensitivity, inspiration are of the essence. All this is true in a sense, but it doesn't help much because it defines the great teacher, and in terms rather like those which might be used to define the great poet. Teacher education has to be seen on an analogy with the creative writing course, not of Coleridge, Wordsworth and their circle.

Again, informal teaching is based on the assumption that the relationship between teacher and taught is primarily a personal one, even a discipleship, rather than a contractual one. Responsiveness to and affection for children is the child-centred expression of this. The *right* of the teacher to get angry is the middle-of-the-road one. The defender of corporal punsihment who claims to act out of love and care – and the claim is often made – is taking basically the same stance.

The authority of the older generation over the younger is being questioned and with it the authority of teacher over pupil. The informal teacher, dedicted to charisma rather than contract, is prepared to concede ground in claiming to be '*in* authority' so long as he can maintain his claim to be '*an* authority', the man of knowledge, the master of content. For he can use knowledge as control, finessing the residual potentials for confrontation by informalizing them – conning the kids.

My characterization is a mere thumbnail sketch and does less than justice to the pragmatic power of such a position. In teacher education acceptance of informality in this sense leads to the failure to relate the development of the student and the development of his skills; for the assumption is that techniques can be independently integrated by each student by virtue of the organizing power of his personality. Teaching becomes expression of self rather than enabling of others. And in the last analysis the quality of the person is taken to determine the quality of the teacher.

Formal teaching is based upon the assumption that teaching can be developed experimentally as an art in which the logic of content and the logic of form are in dialectic tension. It is the form – as in sonata or blues – which supports the development. Pedagogy is the playing out of the improvisation within a form in the classroom. The critique of pedagogy is complex, and under discussion. My own view is that the central problem is the teaching of error as problems of control drag the teacher inexpert in his form off course.

This view implies that teaching is a professional skill in performance; and – within limits of course – teachers less than satisfactory as people, uncertain in their beliefs and fragmentary in their knowledge, can practise their art to the great and lasting advantage of their pupils, while the rare exemplars of perfection who may be attracted into teaching will also profit, as teachers, from the discipline of form. Note too that the implication of experimental teaching within forms is that the adoption of styles of teaching should be experimental. I want to emphasize this. Were it not so common, I should find it incredible that teachers make up their minds how to teach on some *a priori* basis and then refuse to experiment with a range of forms.

In formal teaching, the relationship between teacher and taught is primarily a contractual one. It *can* be personal, but only if the personal tone of the relationship is not used to smoothe the way to slackness of contract. Anything which might lead a pupil to forgive you for failing to teach him more effectively is to be avoided. When rights and duties are being satisfied, a sure foundation has been laid. The teacher exercises his skill to the full advantage of the child he dislikes as of the child he likes.

In a reassessment of authority the formal teacher will prefer to stand by his position '*in* authority', giving him a legitimate responsibility for good order and disciplined learning in his classroom as the basis of his contract. He will be prepared to make realistic concessions with respect to his claims as '*an* authority' recognizing himself as one who does not represent public knowledge, but rather manages people's encounters with it. In that sense, he will stress his role as a man of learning rather than a man of knowledge, as an informed seeker rather than an authority for the validation of knowledge.

Curriculum research, artistry and teaching[*]

Experience tells me that, if I am not to be misunderstood, I must begin this paper by offering you a brief sketch of my views on the relation of research to educational action. These views are set out at a greater length in other work which I do not necessarily expect this audience to be familiar with (Stenhouse 1979a, 1979b, 1980).

First, I should mention that there is in England a strong doctrine that the study of education is fed by the contributory disciplines of history, philosophy, and sociology. I agree that these disciplines do contribute to our understanding of education. In my own personal experience I can say that in the curriculum project with which I am most closely associated, the Humanities Curriculum Project, my own contribution was substantially influenced by my knowledge of the history of elementary school readers, of the philosophical work of R.S. Peters, of the social psychology of groups and of the sociology of knowledge.

However, these disciplines, while they serve to stimulate educational imagination and to define the conditions of educational action, do not serve to guide such action. They provide for education – as rules of the game and traditions of play do for a sport – a context in which to plan intelligent action. But they do not tell us how to act.

The yearning towards a form of research which might guide educational action led educational researchers to look enviously at agricultural research. Here, in a tradition associated with Ronald Fisher, researchers had conducted field trials which utilized random sampling in block and plot designs in order to recommend to farmers those strains of seed and crop treatments which would maximize yield. Both random sampling – which legitimized the deployment of

* 'Artistry and teaching: the teacher as the focus of research and development': paper given at the Summer Institute on Teacher Education, Simon Fraser University, Vancouver, 1980; published in D. Hopkins and M. Wideen (eds) *Alternative Perspectives on School Improvement* Falmer Press, 1984.

the statistics of probability to estimate error and significance – and measure of yield presented problems in educational research. A number of classic papers, among which Campbell and Stanley's 'Experimental and quasi-experimental designs for research in teaching' (1963) is prominent, have considered the robustness of various experimental designs and statistical procedures in terms of reliability and validity as sampling falls away from the desideratum of randomness. The doctrine of behavioural objectives allied to the development of criterion-referenced testing was developed to give a measure of educational yield.

Personally, I am satisfied that the application of this so-called 'psycho-statistical paradigm' (Fienberg, 1977) in educational research provides no reliable guide to action (though it may contribute a little to theory). It has to assume, as agriculturists assume in treating a crop in a field, consistency of treatment throughout the treatment group; but it is the teacher's job to work like a gardener rather than a farmer, differentiating the treatment of each subject and each learner as the gardener does each flower bed and each plant. The variability of educational situations is grossly underestimated: sampling procedures cannot be related to educational action except on a survey basis rather than an experimental basis. Further, behavioural objectives are quite inappropriate to education except in the case of skill learning. They are a monument to the philosophical naïveté of a psychological traditon which could simplify intentionality and purpose as 'having a goal'. Purpose in education is about having an agenda.

Now, if I am right about this – and you will not readily persuade me that I am not – then the question arises: if experimental research based on sampling cannot tell us how to act in education, how are we as teachers to know what to do?

One answer to this question is that instructions shall be laid down for us in the form of curricula and specifications of teaching methods. I reject this. Education is learning in the context of a search for truth. Truth cannot be defined by the State even through democratic processes: close control of curricula and teaching methods in schools is to be likened to the totalitarian control of art. Reaching towards the truth through education is a matter of situational professional judgement; and professors of education or administrators cannot tell us what we should be doing. Prescriptions will vary according to cases. You don't need a doctor at all if he is going to give you a treatment laid down by the State or suggested by his professor without bothering to examine you and make a diagnosis.

Educational action is concerned with varying according to case and to context the pursuit of truth through learning. In this subtle and complicated process, how is the teacher to conceive the problem: what shall I do? This riddle provides the context and occasion of my paper.

*   *   *   *   *

The student who, during the course of ten years in school, meets two or three outstanding and congenial teachers has had a fortunate educational experience. Many are not so lucky.

The improvement of schooling hinges on increasing the numbers of outstanding teachers, on serving their needs, and on trying to ensure that their virtues are not frustrated by the system. The basic institutional frameworks of the educational enterprise – the neighbourhood elementary school and the comprehensive high school – are for the moment stably established or well on the way. Within these frameworks it is the outstanding teachers who transmute the process of instruction into the adventure of education. Others, it is true, may teach us; but it is they who teach us to delight in learning and to exult in the extension of powers learning gives us.

As part of a National Science Foundation study of the status of science education in United States schools, Bob Stake and Jack Easley of the University of Illinois directed a collection of *Case Studies in Science Education* (1978). Eleven close case studies of high schools and their feeder elementaries in different States were followed up by a national survey. One of their major conclusions confirmed the stance I have just taken. The science teaching that students received was good to the extent that they met good science teachers: teachers who, being interested in science, were absorbed by and skilful in teaching it.

That good teaching is created by good teachers may to some of you seem self-evident to the point of absurdity. You don't need eleven case studies across the American nation – or me to fly to Vancouver from Norwich – to tell you that. But the implications of this self-evident proposition do not seem to be widely grasped.

Good teachers are necessarily autonomous in professional judgement. They do not need to be told what to do. They are not professionally the dependents of researchers or superintendents, of innovators or supervisors. This does not mean that they do not welcome access to ideas created by other people at other places or in other times. Nor do they reject advice, consultancy or support. But they do know that ideas and people are not of much real use until they are digested to the point where they are subject to the teacher's own judgement. In short, it is the task of all educationalists outside the classroom to serve the teachers; for only they are in the position to create good teaching.

Let me restate my case by saying that I am declaring teaching an art, and then elaborate on that.

By an art I mean an exercise of skill expressive of meaning. The painter, the poet, the musician, the actor and the dancer all express meaning through skill. Some artists fly so high that we designate them geniuses, and that may be true of some teachers. But a claim as ambitious as that does not need to be made on behalf of the outstanding teachers I have spoken of. It is enough that they have assiduously cultivated modest but worthwhile talents like those of the innumerable stonemasons who adorned the English parish churches or those sound repertory actors who exceed in number the jobs the theatre has to offer. In short I am not elevating teachers inordinately. Rather I am diagnosing the nature of their job in order to discern how performances may be improved. I'm suggesting that just as dramatists, theatre school staff, producers, stage managers, front of house managers and even booking agencies need to understand to some degree the players' art, so curriculum developers, educational researchers, teacher educators, supervisors and administrators need to understand the art of the teacher.

Teaching is the art which expresses in a form accessible to learners an understanding of the nature of that which is to be learned. Thus, teaching music is about understanding the nature of music and having the skill to teach it true to one's understanding. Teaching tennis is about understanding the logic and psychology and techniques of the game and about expressing that understanding through skill in teaching. Similarly, the teaching of French expresses an understanding of the nature of language and culture and of that particular language and culture; the teaching of wrought ironwork as a craft expresses the relationship of material to fitness for use and to concepts of beauty; and so forth. And one mainstream tradition of teaching is an expression of knowledge of a discipline or field such as history, science or geography. To teach such a discipline or field of knowledge is always to 'teach' the epistemology of that discipline, the nature of its tenure on knowledge.

My own belief, as I have said, is that whether teaching is concerned with that knowledge we associate with the disciplines or with arts or with practical skills, it should aspire to express a view of knowledge or of a field of activity. This epistemological desideratum might be expressed by saying that the teacher should aspire to give learners access to insight into the status of what they learn. The way towards this is that a view of knowledge comes to infuse the teacher's perception of subject matter and judgement of the performance of students, and that this view and its status becomes revealed by teaching to the student. Such a perception of knowledge develops and deepens throughout the career of a good teacher and it is the product of the teacher's personal construction or reconstruction of knowledge. It can be assisted by reading and instruction, but it is essentially a personal construction created from socially available resources and it cannot be imparted by others or to others in a straightforward manner.

Now, the construction of a personal perception of our world from the knowledge and traditions that our culture makes available to us is a task that faces not only the teacher, but also the student, and teaching rests on both partners in the process being at different stages of the same enterprise. This is clear to us when we watch a great musician teaching a master class, but it tends to be obscured in schools in the ordinary classroom. The technical claptrap of learning systems and behavioural objectives is much to blame for this. Good learning is about making, not mere doing. It is about constructing a view of the world. It is not about showing that, although you have failed in that construction, you are capable of all the performances that would appear to make the constuction possible. Education is for real: it is not about practice shots.

Let me sum up so far by an analogy (which is not to be pursued too far). The art of social comedy expresses a view of manners and morals as people live them: the art of education expresses a view of knowledge as people live it. The medium of one is theatrical entertainment; of the other, schooling. Both are at their highest when the audience or learner is brought to reflect consciously on the message he receives. This fulfilment depends not only upon the quality of the play or the curriculum, but also upon the art of the actor or teacher.

And now let me take a second step. All good art is an enquiry and an experiment. It is by virtue of being an artist that the teacher is a researcher. The point appears to be difficult to grasp because education faculties have been invaded by the idea that research is scientific and concerned with general laws. This notion persists even though our universities teach music and literature and history and art and lay an obligation on their staff in these fields to conduct research. There is no reason why research in education should look to science.

The artist is the researcher *par excellence*. So much so that prominent scientists are now arguing that, while routine consolidation in science can be achieved by following conventional scientific method, the big breakthroughs really show that science is an art. I'm sceptical of that, but I am clear that all art rests upon research and the purpose of the artist's research is to improve the truth of his performance. Leonardo's sketchbooks, George Stubbs dissecting a horse in his studio, Nureyev working with a partner in a new ballet, Solti and the Chicago Symphony Orchestra tackling Beethoven, Derek Jacobi evolving his Hamlet, all are engaged in enquiry, in research and development of their own work. And this development, although it involves improvement of technique, is not for the sake of technique: it is for the sake of the expression of a truth in a performance which challenges criticism in those terms.

Thus an elementary school teacher who wishes to improve his or her teaching of science will record teaching or invite a colleague in as observer, and will, if possible, bring in an outsider to monitor the children's perceptions as a basis for 'triangulation'. From this the next aspiration is to drop the outsider and move towards open discourse between teacher and children about the teaching/learning process in the classroom and its 'meaning'. A crucial aspect of this meaning is the impression of science – always expressed in specific instances or episodes – that the children are acquiring. And this the teacher needs to criticize in the light of the philosophy of science. All teaching falsifies its subject as it shapes it into the form of teaching and learning: the art of pedagogy is to minimize the falsification of knowledge. It is the aspiration to do this, to shape understanding without distortion into pedagogic forms, that is the challenge to develop one's art.

Now, if you say that most teachers are not like this, I shall reply that some are, and that it is the model of teaching that those teachers display to us that we need to disseminate. . . . The way ahead is to disseminate the idea of teacher as artist with the implication that artists exercise autonomy of judgement founded upon research directed towards the improvement of their art. The changes in school administration or curriculum or teaching arrangements which will be required are those which make it possible to implement that vision.

If I, as a teacher, absorb and accept the case I have just been putting, then it is clear to me that I am the focus of research and development. Who else could be? My problem then is how to get others to recognize it. That is not going to be too easy. If teachers are at the bottom of the pile, there are bound to be lots of people who like it that way. So, though I can exercise my art in secret, or even in a small group of consenting adults, if I want the support of a movement, I need to make alliances and develop some political power.

Let me give you a short account of the kinds of support that have been developed round the teacher-as-researcher movement in Britain. First, there is an alliance between some universities or colleges of education and some teacher groups. What is required of the universities is that they break the stranglehold of the 'psycho-statistical and nomothetic paradigm' on educational research. The universities which have done this recognize forms of research alternative to the still dominant tradition of scientific positivism with its emphasis on experimental and survey procedures conducted on samples in field settings and giving rise to 'results'. Among these alternative forms are experimental or descriptive case studies which may be based upon the teacher's access either to the classroom as a laboratory or to the school or classroom as a setting for participant observation. In Britain standards for these research paradigms are now in process of being worked out at master's and doctoral levels, both through discussion at conferences and in the consultations between internal and external examiners.

This alliance with universities is important for the teachers because it gives access to a pattern of part-time study right up to the level of doctorate which turns one towards one's professional work rather than away from it and offers a systematic training in the appropriate research skills as well as a grasp of the theoretical issues applicable to close-in, practitioner research. This tradition, once established at advanced levels, begins to influence patterns of in-service work.

Academic validation has drawn on alternative traditions which include the hermeneutic tradition and the neo-Marxist tradition from Germany, phenomenology and ethnomethodology. These theoretical currents are in harmony with reappraisals at present being conducted in the social science community whose interests lie outside education. This link is a source of validation and alliance. It turns the education faculty towards sociologists, anthropologists and historians as alternative allies to psychologists and philosophers. This shift of alliance has, of course, profound power implications in the academic community.

The academic endorsement of styles of research into schooling which are as accessible to practising school teachers as to university teachers and professional researchers can also, of course, create considerable hostility and fear among university faculty. In my view, this is misplaced. The universities can only thrive as a result of an extension of the boundaries of the research community. The shift is from lecturing on research results towards training researchers. The message is that the 'role' of universities is bound to be central in the development of a tradition that puts research at its heart.

Of course, teacher power expresses itself in unfamiliar ways within this tradition. The Schools Council for Curriculum and Examinations, the main funding agency for curriculum in Britain, recently funded a conference of teachers on 'The Teacher as Researcher' (Nixon, 1981).

The teachers who organized it did not invite anyone from a university. I guess we talk too much, and they wanted time to think over the issues in their own way. But they will need us. And we need them. In an age of accountability educational research will be held accountable for its relevance to practice, and that relevance can only be validated by practitioners.

Enlightened administrators look benevolently on the teacher-researcher model of staff development, and one can gather support there. The idea has potential appeal for teacher unions, though that hasn't really been pressed home in Britain. One way or another there are the makings of a movement.

But what are the consequences to be expected of such a movement if it gathers momentum and power? May we expect teachers to demand schools fit for educational artist-researchers to live in? And what would those look like?

We can only guess. But I am suggesting that forms of schooling can best be seen as obsolescent when they constrict developments in teaching. I believe that the development of the teacher as artist means that some time in the future we are going to have to get rid of school principals. My own guess is that we shall need delegatory rather than legislative democracy. Committees will not decide what to do: artists grudge that use of time. They will delegate the power to decide to individuals for fixed periods and will hold them accountable. In the university in which I work professors' duties are no different from those of lecturers: a professorship is more an award than an appointment. A capacity for intellectual leadership is appropriate, but the leadership role is not structured on the job. Perhaps we need such professors in schools: persons appointed by their colleagues to a status which recognizes their distinctive capacity to contribute to the community of teachers.

A community of teachers whose attention is primarily focused on the art of teaching will require – as a company of actors does or as a university faculty does – an administrative support structure. It is important that the teacher who acts as president of the school faculty commands the highest salary in the institution, and that below that the head of the administration has parity with the highest grade of teacher. It is vital that the adminstration service teaching, not lead it.

However, we shall not change teaching by creating a school organized on that model. The reform of school organization needs to be an adjustment to the development of teaching. It is the teacher who is focus of research and development: only the teacher himself can change the teacher himself. You can reorganize schools and he can remain as he was. You can pull down the walls and make an open school; but open teaching remains an achievement of the teacher's art, and an achievement that is an expression of understanding.

What are the implications of all this for in-service development?

My position is that in-service development must be the development of the teacher as artist. That means the development of understanding expressed in performance: understanding of the nature of knowledge expressed in the art form of teaching and learning. No skills unless they enhance understanding, no curriculum study unless it enhances understanding, no courses of study unless they enhance understanding, no assessment unless it enhances understanding. What I am advocating is so radical that I may not be communicating it. Let me sharpen the message in the area of curriculum: I am saying that the purpose of any curriculum change, any curriculum research, any curriculum development is the enhancement of the art of teaching, of understanding expressed as performance. The idea that you want a change and the change is dependent on retraining teachers is a non-starter.

As a starting-point teachers must want change, rather than others wanting to change them. That means that the option of professional development leading towards professional satisfaction of a kind that brings an enhancement of self must be made clear and open to teachers.

Teachers have been taught that teaching is instrumental but improving education is not about improving teaching as a delivery system. Crucial is the desire of the artist to improve his art. This art is what the experienced teacher brings to in-service development. Good in-service education recognizes and strengthens the power and primacy of that art. It offers curricula to teachers as music in-service offers Beethoven or Stravinsky to musicians – to further the art. In-service is linked to change because art is about change and only develops in change. If the art of teaching could develop without change, then there would be no need for change in education. It is art's appetite for change that makes educational change necessary to the virtue of schooling.

The artist is the researcher whose enquiry expresses itself in performance of his art rather than (or as well as) in a research report. In an essentially practical art like education all the research and all the in-service education we offer should support that research towards performance on the part of the teacher. For there is in education no absolute and unperformed knowledge. In educational research and scholarship the ivory towers where the truth is neglected are so many theatres without players, galleries without pictures, music without musicians. Educational knowledge exists in, and is verified or falsified in, its performance.

References

CAMPBELL, D.T. and STANLEY, J.C. (1963) 'Experimental and quasi-experimental designs for research on teaching' in N.L. Gage (ed.) *A Handbook of Research on Teaching* Chicago: Rand McNally.

FIENBERG, S.E. (1977) The collection and analysis of ethnographic data in educational research *Anthropology and Education Quarterly* 8, 2, 50–7.

NIXON, J. (ed.) (1981) *A Teacher's Guide to Action Research: Evaluation, Enquiry and Development in the Classroom* London: Grant McIntyre.

STAKE, R.E. and EASLEY, J. (1978) *Case Studies in Science Education Vol I: The Case Reports; Vol II: Design, Overview and General Findings* Washington, D.C.: Superintendent of Documents, US Government Printing Office (Stock nos. 038–000–00377–1, 038–000–00376–3).

STENHOUSE, L. (1979a) 'Using research means doing research' in H. Dahl, A. Lysne and P. Rand (eds) *A Spotlight on Educational Problems* Festskrift for Johannes Sandven, Oslo University Press.

STENHOUSE, L. (1979b) 'Research as a basis for teaching': inaugural lecture in the University of East Anglia, published in L. Stenhouse (1983) *Authority, Education and Emancipation* Heinemann Educational Books.

STENHOUSE, L. (1980) Curriculum research and the art of the teacher *Curriculum* 1, 1, 40–4.

Section 3

Rationale

Research underlines the provisionality of knowledge. Teaching, at every level, is vulnerable if it does not acknowledge that error is a realistic intellectual achievement and failure a realistic practical achievement, for a critical appreciation of error and failure is a necessary foundation for improvement. Research, which disciplines curiosity and calls certainty into question, is a proper basis for teaching.

J.R. & D.H.

RESEARCH AS A BASIS FOR TEACHING*

Fortuitously, this year is the nine hundredth anniversary of the birth of a man commonly regarded as the forefather of the tradition of rational speculation in western universities: Peter Abélard. His world was, of course very different from ours, and it is one which I am not competent to re-create. But it is part of my thesis that all human knowledge has about it an element of error, and I may perhaps adopt Abélard as a source for my learning even though I am not true to his teaching.

He was of course a great dialectician, and by virtue of this a great teacher. We should say today that his research field was dialectics and that it fed directly into his teaching.

'It is,' he wrote, 'one thing to enquire into truth by deliberation but quite another to make ostentation the end of all disputation for while the first is devoted to study which strives to edify, the second is but the mere impulse of pride which seeks only for self glory. By the one we set out to learn the wisdom which we do not possess: by the other we parade the learning which we trust is ours' (Sikes, 1965: 55). To call for research-based teaching is, I suggest, to ask us as teachers to share with our pupils or students the process of our learning the wisdom which we do not possess so that they can get into critical perspective the learning which we trust is ours.

Research-based teaching is more demanding than teaching which offers instruction through a rhetoric of conclusions. Abélard (1972: 18–19) tells us that he slipped from one to the other under the distraction of his love for Heloise.

In measure as this passionate rapture absorbed me more and more, I devoted ever less time to philosophy and to the work of the school. Indeed it became loathsome to me to go to the school or to linger there: the labour,

* 'Research as a basis for teaching': inaugural lecture, University of East Anglia, February 1979, published in L. Stenhouse *Authority, Education and Emancipation* Heinemann Educational Books, 1983.

moreover, was very burdensome since my nights were vigils of love and my days of study. My lecturing became utterly careless and lukewarm: I did nothing because of inspiration, but everything merely as a matter of habit. I had become nothing more than a reciter of my former discoveries, and though I still wrote poems, they dealt with love, not with the secrets of philosophy.

My colleague, Professor Malcolm Bradbury, has hinted fictionally that some modern dons may have like problems, though their diaries in the *Times Higher Education Supplement* appear to claim that travel and administration outweigh even family and television as contemporary distractors.

The idea that research is a necessary basis for good teaching is not universally admitted – much less practised – even in universities. Joseph Ben-David (1977), reviewing *Centres of Learning* for the Carnegie Commission on Higher Education, provides an excellent statement of a contrary position. Addressing the difficulty of reconciling research and teaching, he regards the competing demands on time and effort as only a superficial impediment, and reaches after a more fundamental conflict. He suggests that 'knowledge that can be taught no longer requires investigation, while knowledge that still needs to be investigated cannot yet be taught' and he claims that 'teaching requires a body of established authoritative knowledge.'

Now, Abélard worked in the context of a 'body of established authoritative knowledge' far more secure than most of us could recognize today: the Scriptures, the writings of the Fathers of the Church, and the authority of the Church itself; and this was not an authority he questioned. Yet his position was almost the opposite of that taken by Ben-David. Established authoritative knowledge hardly required teaching; it was embodied in the Church or was a matter of mere instruction. Teaching was required where doubt or bewilderment caused by obscurity or apparent contradiction in the authorities required clarification by dialectic. His aim was understanding as a fortification, but not the ground, of faith, for he conceded that the final mysteries were inscrutable. Christian doctrine, the knowledge of God and His ways attainable by human beings, was for Abélard 'essentially rational and logical, and . . . it lay within the province of human thought' (Sikes, 1965: 50). Whenever appeal to the authority of the Church and its tradition left space for interpretation and hence for error – called 'heresy' – there was space for research and hence for non-authoritative teaching. The teacher could not, of course, claim to be an authority without offence to the power of the Church.

Only in the presence of doubt is teaching called for, one might gather from Abélard. Only that which has the warrant of certainty can be taught, Ben-David answers. And he can relate his view to the one I have represented by Abélard (Ben-David, 1977: 94–5):

> In . . . relatively closed traditions of higher learning, combining research with teaching presented no difficulty since the difference between elementary and advanced knowledge was not one of substance or certainty, but one of mastery. Original research consisted of novel interpretation or systematization of the tradition and could be done as part of the organization of the material for teaching. For academic teachers in the humanities the ideal of their being original investigators was not a nineteenth-century innovation. The university had been a seat of creative scholarship in philosophy throughout the Middle Ages, and many universities continued to employ original scholars throughout the seventeenth and eighteenth centuries.

This is to attribute the difficulty in reconciling research and teaching to the nineteenth-century development in research in which the German universities were leaders and of which we are all heirs. In this development the pioneer field was history with its attendant technical studies such as philology, palaeography, diplomacy and archaeology. Behind history came the natural sciences and later the social sciences.

Now the environment of research in this new tradition was not the lecture hall where the speculative disputation might be conducted, but the archive, the library, the laboratory or the field site. Research became collaborative by virtue of the network of journals and the talk in coffee-breaks, but the actual activity was conducted in private. It had become industrialized. The steel-rolling mill is not open to inspection as the local blacksmith is. In place of the speculative disputation open to the student as participant observer, enquiry was expressed in the archive search or the series of laboratory experiments, mute occupations whose meaning was not self-explanatory to the observer.

Ben-David contributes an interesting analysis of the problems of keeping research and teaching in mutual and fortifying interaction, and concludes that by the end of the nineteenth century 'the implement-ation of the ideal posed serious problems'. To these the American graduate school was one response, associating research-based teaching with the training of professional researchers. Ben-David's diagnosis of the post-war situation is not encouraging (1977: 124):

> There have been no serious efforts at constructive restructuring of the relationship between research and teaching. . . . The resulting frustrations have reinforced the long-standing trend towards the transfer of the seat of advanced research from the universities to non-teaching research institutions.

The Centre for Applied Research in Education was founded by this university in 1970, initially as a non-teaching research institution within a university setting. The fact that we have developed a graduate teaching programme on the basis of the resultant research activity has prompted me to address the problems explored in this lecture.

The knowledge we teach in universities is won through research; and I have come to believe that such knowledge cannot be taught correctly except through some form of research-based teaching. The grounds for this belief are epistemological. Knowledge of the kind we have to offer is falsified when it is presented as the results of research detached from an understanding of the research process which is warrant for those results.

Abélard has a lot to teach us here, for he is correct in his under-standing that what is represented as authoritative, and established independently of scholarly warrant, cannot be knowledge. It is faith. What is unquestionable is unverifiable and unfalsifiable. It may be true belief, but it is not knowledge in the sense in which we in universities deal with it or are equipped to deal with it. Our know-ledge is questionable, verifiable and differentially secure. Unless our students understand that, what they take from us is error: the error that research yields established authoritative knowledge. That this error is widespread must be apparent to anyone who has listened to the questions asked of academics by laymen on television. And if we educate teachers who will transmit this error to their pupils, the error will continue to be widespread. We shall support by our teaching the idea that faith in authority is an acceptable substitute for grasp of the grounds of knowledge, even perhaps a substitute for faith in God. Once the Lord spoke to man: now scientists tell us that. . . .

This epistemological falsification in teaching research-based know-ledge authoritatively is compounded by a simple error. We in the course of our research have made and witnessed a large number of audio and video-recordings of teaching, and we find it virtually impossible to locate passages of authoritative exposition by lecture which are not criticized by observers, who are as well-qualified as the lecturer, on the grounds that they contain errors of fact or indefensible judgements. And these shortcomings are perceptible to only a small proportion of students. This intrusion of error into exposition and instruction is not surprising, nor is it a serious criticism of teachers as scholars. The archetypal effort to compress and present knowledge in accessible form, the encyclopaedia, encounters the same prob-lem, for all the resources at the disposal of its editors (See Einbinder, 1964)

No teacher of normal endowments can teach authoritatively without lending his authority to errors of fact or of judgement. But my case goes deeper than that. Were the teacher able to avoid this, he would, in teaching knowledge as authoritative, be teaching an unacceptable proposition about the nature of knowledge: that its warrant is to be found in the appeal to the expertise of persons rather than in the appeal to rational justification in the light of evidence. I believe that most teaching in schools and a good deal in universities promotes that error. The schooled reveal themselves as uneducated when they look towards knowledge for the reassurance of authoritative certainty rather than for the adventure of speculative understanding.

How to teach a different lesson is an educational problem of considerable technical difficulty. Even though education be voluntary – and it is largely not so – the act of will by which a person devotes himself to a sustained and arduous course is not easy to maintain. The teacher is not concerned simply with the justification of knowledge. He needs to motivate and to set up social situations conducive to work. Leadership is necessary, authority is inescapable. The problem is how to design a practicable pattern of teaching which maintains authority, leadership and the responsibility of the teacher, but does not carry the message that such authority is the warrant of knowledge.

This problem is not unlike that of explaining to a naive person with no experience of our world that a television set does not make pictures but transmits images of things taking place outside itself. The view of knowledge that one can get in a classroom or lecture theatre is most often comparable to that offered by the television set: Plato's simile of the cave holds even if we do not locate reality in ideal forms. Taught knowledge is a shadow or picture of knowledge rather than knowledge as it is apprehended by the researcher who creates or discovers it.

This problem of the relationship of the authority of the teacher to the representation of knowledge in teaching has been a central theme of my own work and that of some of my colleagues in the Centre for Applied Research in Education. In the jargon of our field it is the problem of enquiry- or discovery-based teaching or of teaching through discussion. To my mind the essence of the problem is expressed by declaring the aim of teaching in its fullest ambition to be: to develop an understanding of the problem of the nature of knowledge through an exploration of the provenance and warrant of the particular knowledge we encounter in our field of study. Any education which does not achieve this leaves its recipients disadvantaged as compared with those who have followed courses where it is achieved: for we are talking about the insight which raises mere competence and possession of information to intellectual power of a kind which can emancipate.

On this occasion I do not want to get trapped in the details of educational research. Rather I shall confine myself to three specific problems encountered by those attempting research-based teaching in the sense I have given it. They are: the need to cover ground in a subject; the psychological barriers to this kind of teaching; and the interpretation of the idea of research-based teaching in relation to the practice of primary and secondary schools.

The problem of coverage is generally formulated by asserting that discovery and discussion are such slow procedures for learning that the need for a quantity of information precludes their use. If we are to cover the curriculum we set ourselves, we must resort to instruction.

Of course we need instruction. And textbooks too. The key is that the aim of discovery and discussion is to promote understanding of the nature of the concessions to error that are being made in that part of our teaching where we rely upon instruction or textbooks. The crucial difference is between an educated and an uneducated use of instruction. The educated use of instruction is sceptical, provisional, speculative in temper. The uneducated use mistakes information for knowledge. Information is not knowledge until the factor of error, limitation or crudity in it is appropriately estimated, and it is assimilated to structures of thinking – disciplines (Hirst, 1965), realms of meaning (Phenix, 1964), modes of experience (Oakeshott, 1933) – which give us the means of understanding.

Two parallel activities need to be pursued: instruction, which gives us access to conclusions which represent in simplified and hence distorted form our best grasp of a realm of knowledge and meaning, and learning by enquiry or discovery, which enables us to understand how to utilize such a representation of knowledge, to assess its limitations and to develop the means of pushing outwards beyond these limitations.

The interaction between enquiry and instruction is perhaps best understood through a concrete instance. A person of my acquaintance is practising as a non-graduate research worker in biochemistry in a government research agency and at the same time taking an undergraduate degree in the Open University. At once, therefore, a professional researcher and an undergraduate, this student is advantaged as compared with those not engaged in research by the clearer perception of the status and use of textbook knowledge made possible by research experience. The justification of research as a basis for learning or for teaching is the perspective to be gained from the hill of enquiry over the plain of knowledge.

But more than this, the seeker, the questioner, the researcher, is always at an advantage *vis-à-vis* the person who claims to be a knower; hence, the dramatic structure of Plato's dialogues. One can combine enquiry-learning and instruction appropriately only by using the enquiry to teach the student to question the instruction.

Herein lies the psychological barrier to research-based teaching. It may leave me *in* authority, but it asks me to depreciate my claim to be *an* authority (see Peters, 1966). The article on research in the eleventh edition of the *Encyclopaedia Britannica*, the memorial summary of the British perception of knowledge on the threshold of the First World War, observes that 'Investigations of every kind which have been based on original sources of knowledge may be styled "research", and it may be said that without 'research' no authoritative works have been written . . .'. The implication is that research, by allowing us to produce authoritative work, makes us authoritative. Such authority is prestigious and highly satisfying personally; but it is vulnerable to the next questioner, and even more so to changes in the paradigm of knowledge. Sir Walter Scott (1906) remarked of the persistence of astrology: 'Grave and studious men were loth to relinquish the calculations which had early become the principal objects of their studies, and felt reluctant to descend from the predominating height to which a supposed insight . . . had exalted them over the rest of mankind.' (Kuhn, 1970)

The psychological reluctance to abandon the claim to be an authority is reinforced by fear of the implications for the social order, where such authority holds heirarchy in place – as my colleague, Professor Robert Ashton perceives: 'Like the schoolmaster, the university don, the householder, the civil magistrate and the King himself, the master (of apprentices) wields an authority which is in essence paternalistic and contributes to the maintenance of order in society as a whole' (Ashton, 1978: 9).

Our deep psychological and social needs for that conception of knowledge which makes the elders curators of truth are yet further reinforced by our need as teachers for institutional authority in the schools and universities in which we work. As Derek Morrell and John Witherington wrote in their Schools Council Working Paper on the *Raising of the School Leaving Age* (1968) – from which our Humanities Curriculum Project sought its validation: 'If the teacher emphasizes in the classroom his common humanity with the pupils, and his common uncertainty in the face of many problems, the pupils will not take kindly to being demoted to the status of children in other relationships within the same institution.'

In authority-based teaching the teacher is Promethean: in research-based teaching the teacher evokes a Promethean response from the student, who casts his master in the role of Hephaestus. In teaching there is always a retaining of power as well as a conferring of power. Research-based teaching, conceived as enquiry-based teaching, shifts the balance of power towards the student. It is his own research or enquiry which gives the teacher the strength to do this . Yet it happens that, fathering an Oedipus, the teacher is tempted to expose him to destroy him.

These are difficult matters, and most of us go for compromises; but they are compromises charged nonetheless with the emotions aroused by the extremes. I claim no more than that a research base offers the teacher a security for his authority in a mastery of seeking rather than of knowing, and hence provides him with a necessary protection in the enterprise of educating those who will, he wants to hope, exceed his grasp.

The view of knowledge and teaching which I have outlined seems at first sight to apply to universities, but not to schools. This is not a limitation I accept. Research may be broadly defined as systematic enquiry made public. The enquiry should, I think, be rooted in acutely felt curiosity, and research suffers when it is not. Such enquiry becomes systematic when it is structured over time by continuities lodged in the intellectual biography of the researcher and coordinated with the work of others through the cumulative capacity of the organization of the discipline or the subject.

Systematic enquiry of this sort – or approximation to it – is a pattern of learning by a thoughtful study of problems. Such study becomes research when it is made public by being published, at which point the student makes a claim intended to evoke a critical response: that the reported enquiry has resulted in a contribution to knowledge, being soundly based and in some sense new.

Saving only this final stage of publication such enquiry is possible as a basis for learning at quite early stages of education. When it takes place the teacher is not an instructor but instead takes the critical role assigned in fully-blown research to the scholars in the subject who react to publication. And there is no better experience than to work on this pattern with a teacher who has the imagination to initiate enquiry and the judgement to discipline it. The pupils make trials or essays within the enquiry, and the teacher offers an experienced critical reaction.

Thus, when a teacher of six-year-olds separates two children who are fighting and, using them as independent witnesses, invites the class to question them and attempt to reach a judgement concerning the causes of the conflict, that teacher is already equipping those children to understand that the averred causes of the First World War, which they may some day consent to rehearse for 'O'-level history, are not unproblematic. Only such teaching can tend to provide the learner with an acceptable view of accepted knowledge: that is, as questionable knowledge which for present purposes does not need to be questioned.

One of the teachers with whom our Centre is working is known to her pupils in a Dorset middle school as 'the hypothesis teacher', a tribute to her capacity to stimulate hypothetical thinking within the American social studies curriculum, *MAN: A Course of Study*, which, under the inspiration of Jerome Bruner, reached after a framework to support children in an enquiry into the nature of humanness as it can be understood through the study of animal behaviour, anthropology and comparative sociology, set in a context of values. Bruner (1966) spoke of a 'courteous translation' of knowledge into the grasp of children. I think that the courtesy lies in conceding the importance of the right of the learner to speculate, to learn autonomously, to criticize and correct intelligent errors which reach after understanding.

Enquiry-based teaching of this sort necessarily aims at higher levels of attainment than are commonly settled for in schools and it naturally needs the support of instruction. Such instruction is best provided, not through the lecture given by the teacher, but rather through books and audio-visual materials, since this enables the teacher to maintain his critical stance towards the instruction. But the teacher will feel secure in such a role only if he is research-minded to the extent of having an enquiring habit of thought. It will be his task to interpret his claim as a man of knowledge to support his capacity to manage an enquiry towards understanding, 'to legitimize the search' (see Hanley *et al.*, 1970). He must not diminish the importance of that search by suggesting that it can be avoided by appeal to him as an authority who can warrant knowledge.

The teacher's qualification is in that knowledge of which the universities are curators, knowledge based upon enquiry organized as research. Such knowledge celebrates the capacity of the human mind to deal with problems or doubts in at least some areas of human concern, not by a leap of faith, but by a calculated and secure uncertainty. Confronted by the fact that if there is knowledge which is absolute it is, like Abélard's God, finally inscrutable, we settle for serviceable approximations which can be progressively sharpened by sceptical, but systematic, questioning. Only by keeping teaching in touch with enquiry can we do justice to this element in the knowledge we represent.

The university stands – or should stand – behind enquiry in schools as the curator of that uncertainty without which the transmission of knowledge becomes a virtuoso performance in gentling the masses. We do not live up to our principles, of course, but it is of the first importance that we do not rest from trying to do so, routinely from day to day. Whenever we assert and bully with our authority instead of reasoning on an equal base with those we teach and helping them to liberate themselves from our authority as the source of truth, we invite them to faith rather than to knowledge. And our credentials to teach do not support our claiming faith from our students. The university holds no secrets of life and experience except through what Oakeshott (1933) has called 'arrests of experience', the partial perspectives which alone give us a purchase on the limitless universe of experience and hence the possibility of understanding, which we call 'Knowledge'.

We are within reach of Abélard, whose 'statement that our beliefs must be understood does not mean that in his view a complete comprehension of divine matters was possible to men' (Sikes, 1965: 36). But while Abélard's element of uncertainty, constituting as it did a limitation of understanding of the divine, was associated with a sense of deficit, for some of us at least the uncertainty of research-based knowledge is a valued asset. The alternative presents itself, not as the mystical apprehension which supports faith founded in God, but as the threat that certainty will be ideologically based and that truth will be dictated by political authority. It is the thesis of Thrasymachus we oppose.

And since Thrasymachus spoke with the confidence of the practical man, let me at this point, warned by experience, combat what I believe to be a misapprehension about the relation of speculation to action. (I am forewarned of this by criticism of our Humanities Curriculum Project (1970), which sought to offer a speculative style of education through dialectic to those who would leave school at sixteen.) The uncertainty or provisionality of knowledge which I have associated with research is not to be equated with uncertainty of commitment or failure of the will to act. It does not preclude faith or commitment as 'that which we hold firmly in our minds', but rather builds upon it and elucidates it. Commitment needs to be interpreted before it can inform action, and the man of action is more typically he who can act without the reassurance that his interpretation is certain than he who can act only when unafflicted by doubt. Security in uncertainty is the armour which a speculative education can offer. It is a valuable equipment for the practical man.

Not everyone will agree with my analysis of the nature of knowledge and its relation to research and to action. There are those who, agreeing, will judge knowledge dangerous because it gives power to the dipossessed and those who, wishing it were more dangerous, will believe that it lacks the power to break the domination of the hegemony (see Gramsci, 1971). But the achievement of secondary education for all signals, if it does not realize, the aspiration towards a knowledge-based education at every stage of schooling and for everyone – not merely for scholars – and commits the teaching profession to a struggle with the consequences of that ambition.

Historically the great majority of the children of this country have been offered in the state educational system, whether through the elementary school or the secondary modern school, no more than a rudimentary education in the basic skills and such an acquaintance with knowledge as might be expected to inculcate a respect for those who are knowledgeable. Their lot has been to accept that truths are defined by the authority of others. This tradition has lain alongside a tradition among the gentry of knowledge as a mere accomplishment or appurtenance of style. The juxtaposition of these traditions has not merely impaired our capability in the industrial arts, it has also defined scholarship in the liberal disciplines as merely technical, and the results of this are to be observed in the discontent with higher education of many intelligent students, who resist the idea that technical prowess is the precondition of curiosity rather than its servant.

In the familiar tradition the uses of knowledge are reserved for an élite, while the burdens of knowledge are imposed on the generality by an imperious pedagogy. Schools provide students with competences without enhancing their powers. There are gross inequalities in the distribution of the means of thinking, and hence of the power thinking confers, and consequently the creation of a proletariat of the intellect.

To provide an alternative tradition of access to knowledge is a formidable problem for teachers, and it is not a problem to be solved by a change of heart. Important as it may be to declare worthwhile aims for education, good intentions do not pave the way to their fulfilment. What is needed is progress in the art of teaching as a public tradition and a personal achievement.

The character of the art of teaching is to represent to learners through social interaction with them meanings about knowledge. The succession of experiences we provide for them, and within the framework of those experiences the nuances of our questions, our judgements of their work, our tutorial advice, even the very gestures and postures of our bodies, are expressive of those meanings, sometimes explicitly, sometimes as elements in what has come to be called a 'hidden curriculum' (Jackson, 1968). Teaching represents knowledge to people rather as theatre represents life.

Some of those who have called teaching an art appear to think that this suggests it is all flair and no learning. As if actors or dancers or musicians have nothing to learn. Others, on the contrary, imply that it is all skill and can be learned by the imitation of models on the pattern of apprenticeship.

Under the régime of the elementary school, which emphasized a training in skills for pupils, teaching itself could be reduced at the level of minimum competency to a set of skills for pupil teachers. Under such assumptions the training of teachers might be conducted through some sort of apprenticeship, for the masters could do in masterly fashion what the apprentices would be called upon to do. This is not true today. It is not only that the past masters would find themselves inadequate in present classrooms, though I believe this to be true. It is because the act of teaching as a representation of knowledge is inherently problematic.

Teaching which accepts fidelity to knowledge as a criterion can never be judged adequate and rest content. Teachers must be educated to develop their art, not to master it, for the claim to mastery merely signals the abandoning of aspiration. Teaching is not to be regarded as a static accomplishment like riding a bicycle or keeping a ledger; it is, like all arts of high ambition, a strategy in the face of an impossible task.

It is the existence of such vocations with open frontiers for development which provides a basis within the modern university for the second traditional strand in the universities which intertwines with that of liberal education: the professional schools, and among them schools of education. Changes in society, changes in knowledge, related changes in professional role, all contribute to professional doubt and uncertainty, which is confirmed by the experience that old recipes no longer work. And I have argued that the controlled and organized exploitation of such uncertainty in the disciplines of knowledge – the research tradition – is central to the modern university tradition. Research as a strategy is applicable not only to the humanistic and scientific but also to the professional disciplines.

Most of you will have noticed the ambiguity in my title. Just as research in history or literature or chemistry can provide a basis for teaching those subjects, so educational research can provide a basis for teaching and learning about teaching. Professional skill and understanding can be the subject of doubt, that is, of knowledge, and hence of research.

In education what might such research look like?

In this country, since the 1950s, the received doctrine has been that the core of education for teaching lies not in research in education, but in the application to education of the conclusions of research in the 'contributory disciplines' of philosophy, psychology and sociology. Most of those teaching these disciplines to teachers have not been able to share a research base with their students, who are clearly quite unlikely to become philosophers, psychologists, or sociologists, since they are on professional courses for teachers. All too easily philosophers, psychologists and sociologists, whose researches are problematic in their own fields, become – only sometimes against their wishes – authorities in courses for teachers.

An alternative to the constituent disciplines approach is to treat education itself – teaching, learning, running schools and educational systems – as the subject of research. This alternative is not characterized by a neglect of disciplines, upon which it draws eclectically, but rather by the fact that what is drawn from the disciplines and applied to education is not results or even the theories which give shape to each discipline, but methods of enquiry and analysis together with such concepts as have utility for a theory of education. The problems selected for enquiry are selected because of their importance as educational problems, that is, for their significance in the context of professional practice. Research and development guided by such problems will contribute primarily to the understanding of educational action through the construction of a theory of education or a tradition of understanding. Only secondarily will research in this mode contribute to philosophy, psychology or sociology. And this principle of applied research is, I think, appropriate *mutatis mutandis* in all the professional schools of our universities.

How can I best make clear the implications of such a position? Let me take as a point of departure an example of research and training which I take to be sub-professional.

In Ohio State University I visited the Disaster Center, a research and development unit concerned with making more effective the response of the emergency services to disasters. There I saw in a laboratory an exact replica of the Columbus, Ohio, police nerve centre. Police staff were released to man their familiar positions while simulations of disasters were fed through their information channels and their responses were studied. While I was watching, a simulated airplane crash on a Columbus surburb was enacted. It was cleverly contrived. News that the wife of one of the men on the switchboard had just given birth to a son was fed through as a distractor. Information that the deputy superintendent's family had been badly injured when the plane hit his residence invited the team to override public priorities with private ones. Research and training were well integrated. The task was to find the best procedure, to test it against interference and then to enable the emergency team to react smoothly and automatically without needing to pause for thought or run aground on difficult judgements. The laboratory situation was a godsend. You cannot keep crashing planes on Columbus as a research strategy.

If we were to take this as a model for educational research, then we should provide laboratories which simulate classrooms. Desks carefully carved with graffiti might be assembled, walls might be hung with the Fall of Icarus and centrespreads from *The Teachers' World*, fans could pump in the scent of sweat and damp clothes mixed with chalk dust. But what of the pupils?

We deal in education – as with medicine or law or social work – with human action which cannot be channelled through headphones. We need real pupils, and we cannot properly engage them in doubtful experiments or even in placebo treatments.

In short, real classrooms have to be our laboratories, and they are in the command of teachers, not of researchers. This is the characteristic of professional schools: the research act must conform to the obligations of the professional context. This is what we mean by action research. It is a pattern of research in which experimental or research acts cannot be exempted from the demand for justification by professional as well as by research criteria. The teacher cannot learn by enquiry without undertaking that the pupils learn too; the physician cannot experiment without attempting to heal. As the Tavistock Institute put it: 'No therapy without research, no research without therapy' (Smith, 1979).

Such a view of educational research declares that the theory or insights created in collaboration by professional researchers and professional teachers is always provisional, always to be taught in a spirit of enquiry, and always to be tested and modified by professional practice. The teacher who founds his practice of teaching upon research must adopt a research stance to his own practice: it must be provisional and exploratory.

It is this that marks him out as a professional, as compared to the Ohio police emergency team: for while the object of the disaster simulations is to allow them to respond effectively without pausing for thought, the object of educational research is to develop thoughtful reflection in order to strengthen the professional judgement of teachers.

This implies that the educational researcher and the teacher must have a shared language. No doubt there is a need for increasing the research literacy of teachers, but there is also a lot of room for research couched in the vernacular. Here the language of history is a good model: George I instituted professorships of history in 1724 for the purpose of training public servants, and historians still speak of politics in language politicians can understand (see Barzun and Graff, 1977; Hexter, 1972). If we want to influence action, we must have very strong excuses when we abandon the vernacular of action.

It also implies that the teacher be committed to enquiry in the process of his teaching on the grounds that nothing he is offered by teachers of teachers should be accepted on faith. Anyone who doubts this scepticism would do well to study the case of Cyril Burt (Gillie, 1978).

In teaching about teaching, as in teaching about the disciplines of knowledge, we can offer some tips and rules of thumb, but these should not don the mantle of expertise. Moreover, such lore is sub-professional. Professionalism is based upon understanding as a framework of action and understanding is always provisional.

The infusion of teaching by the spirit of enquiry is difficult enough in the context of teaching the disciplines of knowledge. It is even more difficult in professional schools where the natural cry from the fields of professional action is for the reassurance of certainty to ameliorate the agony of responsibility. It is still more difficult in initial training situations, where some are in more need of instruction in clinging to an overturned dinghy than in navigation. But even here the short cut of accepting a 'rhetoric of conclusions' is one we must struggle to avoid. As the McNair Report (1944) said: 'The training of teachers must always be the subject of experiment. It is a growing point of education.' Growing points are uncertainties because uncertainties are potentials. It is the task of universities to keep those potentials open.

The ambition of the programme I have proposed might be understood to remove it from reality. Inaugural lectures in education can too comfortably address the problems of the school in the sky. Not so in this case. I am talking of my everyday practice as an educational researcher and teacher of teachers. But my practice is not successful. Success can be achieved only by lowering our sights. The future is more powerfully formed by our commitment to those enterprises we think it worth pursuing even though we fall short of our aspirations. Abélard's setting out 'to learn the wisdom which we do not possess' commits him, and us who follow him, to the pursuit of an elusive, ever-receding goal. In such an enterprise research is by definition relevant, for its gains accrue, not from a leap towards finality, but from the gradual cumulation of knowledge through the patient definition of error. Its achievement is always provisional, the base camp for the next advance. We shall only teach better if we learn intelligently from the experience of shortfall, both in our grasp of the knowledge we offer and of our knowledge of how to offer it. That is the case for research as a basis for teaching.

References

ABÉLARD, P. *The Story of My Misfortunes (Historia Calamitatum)* translated H.A. Bellows (1972, 1st edition 1922) Macmillan.

ASHTON, R. (1978) *The English Civil War* Weidenfeld & Nicholson.

BARZUN, J. and GRAFF, H.F. (1977 revised edition) *The Modern Researcher* Harcourt Brace Jovanovich.

BEN-DAVID, J. (1977) *Centres of Learning: Britain, France, Germany, United States* McGraw Hill for the Carnegie Commission on Higher Education.

BRUNER, J.S. (1966) *The Process of Education* Harvard University Press.

EINBINDER, H. (1964) *The Myth of the Britannica* MacGibbon & Kee.

Encyclopaedia Britannica (1910, 11th edition).

GILLIE, O. (1978) Sir Cyril Burt and the great IQ fraud *New Statesman*, 24 November, pp. 688–94.

GRAMSCI, A. (1971) *Selections from the Prison Notebooks* edited and translated by O. Hoare and G. Newell Smith (1971) Lawrence & Wishart.

HANLEY, J.P., WHITLA, D.K., MOO, E.M. and WALTER, A.S. (1970) *Curiosity, Competence, Community: Man: A course of Study: An Evaluation* Curriculum Development Associates.

HEXTER, J.H. (1972) *The History Primer* Allen Lane: The Penguin Press.

HIRST, P.H. (1965) 'Liberal education and the nature of knowledge' in R.D. Archambault (ed.) *Philosophical Analysis and Education* Routledge & Kegan Paul.

HUMANITIES CURRICULUM PROJECT (1970) *The Humanities Project: an Introduction* Heinemann Educational Books.

JACKSON, P.W. (1968) *Life in Classrooms* Holt, Rinehart & Winston.

KUHN, T.S. (1970, 2nd edition) *The Structure of Scientific Revolutions* University of Chicago Press.

McNAIR REPORT (1944) *Teachers and Youth Leaders* HMSO (Board of Education non-parliamentary paper).

OAKESHOTT, M. (1933) *Experience and its Modes* Cambridge University Press.

PETERS, R.S. (1966) *Ethics and Education* Allen & Unwin.

PHENIX, P.H. (1964) *Realms of Meaning* McGraw-Hill.

THE SCHOOLS COUNCIL (1965) *Raising the School Leaving Age* (Working Paper No. 2) HMSO.

SCOTT, Sir Walter, (1906) *Guy Mannering* Dent.

SIKES, J.G. (1965, 1st edition 1932) *Peter Abailard* Russell & Russell.

SMITH, D. (1979) 'Action research and the Ford Teaching Project: a strategy for educating classroom practice', unpublished MEd. dissertation, University of Liverpool.

Select bibliography of the work of Lawrence Stenhouse

'Curriculum innovation through a curriculum research project': a working paper prepared for the workshop on the Management of Innovation in Education, organized by the Centre for Educational Research and Innovation (CERI) of OECD, St John's College, Cambridge, July 1969. (Unpublished.)

The Humanities Project: an Introduction Heinemann Educational Books, 1970.

Some limitations of the use of objectives in curriculum research and planning *Paedagogica Europaea* 6, 1970-1, pp. 73–83.

'Problems in curriculum research: a working paper' (with B. MacDonald and J. Rudduck). A paper prepared for an international training seminar organized by the Centre for Applied Research in Education (CARE), University of East Anglia, in cooperation with the Centre for Educational Research and Innovation (CERI) of OECD on the initiative of the Stiftung Volkswagenwerk, 1971. (Unpublished.)

Teaching through small group discussion: formality, rules and authority *Cambridge Journal of Education* 2, 1, 1972, pp. 18–24.

* 'Defining the curriculum problem': a paper given in Norway, 1973, and published in the *Cambridge Journal of Education* 5, 2, 1975, pp. 104–8.

* 'The Humanities Curriculum Project' in H.J. Butcher and H.B. Pont (eds.) *Educational Research in Britain, No. 3* London University Press, 1973, pp. 149–167; reprinted in Lawrence Stenhouse *Authority, Education and Emancipation* Heinemann Educational Books, 1983, pp. 73–89.

* Reproduced in whole or in part in this book.

* *An Introduction to Curriculum Research and Development* Heinemann Educational Books, 1975.

'Neutrality as a criterion in teaching: the work of the Humanities Curriculum Project' in M.J. Taylor (ed.) *Progress and Problems in Moral Education* NFER, 1975, pp. 123–33.

'Problems of research in teaching about race relations' in G.K. Verma and C. Bagley (eds) *Race and Education across Cultures* Heinemann Educational Books, 1975, pp. 305–21.

* 'Teacher development and curriculum design': a paper given at a curriculum conference at the University of Trondheim, Norway, 1975. (Unpublished.)

* 'The measurement results: teaching about race relations – problems and effects': a talk given at a DES conference, July 1976. An edited transcript is reproduced in J. Rudduck *Dissemination of Action Research: Case Record III*. (Unpublished.)

'Design and methods in research in curriculum and teaching': final report of work undertaken on an SSRC personal research grant on Qualitative and Quantitative Approaches to Case Study, no. HR 4001/2, December 1977. (Unpublished.)

* Teachers for all seasons *British Journal of Teacher Education* 3, 3, 1977, pp. 239–42.

* 'Applying research to education', Mimeo, 1978. (Unpublished.)

* 'Culture, attitudes and education': a paper given to the Commonwealth Section of the Royal Society of Arts, 1978; printed in the *Royal Society of Arts Journal* 126, 5268, 1978, pp. 734–45.

* 'Towards a vernacular humanism': a paper given to the Dartington Conference, 1978; printed in the conference proceedings and published in Lawrence Stenhouse *Authority, Education and Emancipation* Heinemann Educational Books, 1983, pp. 163–77.

* 'Can research improve teaching?': a paper given at the Scottish National Conference on Curriculum and Evaluation for PE

teachers, January 1979; printed in *Report: National In-Service Course on Curriculum Design, Course Structure and Evaluation in Physical Education*, Dunfermline college of Physical Education, 1979, pp. 1–4.

* The problem of standards in illuminative research *Scottish Educational Review* 11, 1, 1979, pp. 5–10.

* 'Research as a basis for teaching': inaugural lecture, University of East Anglia, February, 1979; published in L. Stenhouse *Authority, Education and Emancipation* Heinemann Educational Books, 1983, pp. 177–95.

'A study in the dissemination of action research' (with Jean Rudduck): final report to the SSRC, Project HR 3483/1, 1979. (Unpublished.)

* 'Using research means doing research' in H. Dahl, A. Lysne, and P. Rand (eds.), *A Spotlight on Educational Problems* Festskrift for Johannes Sandven, Oslo University Press, 1979, pp. 71–82.

* 'Curriculum knowledge and action: a dialogue' (with Harry Torrance): a paper given at the annual American Educational Research Association Conference, Boston, 1980. (Unpublished.)

* 'Artistry and teaching: the teacher as the focus of research and development': a paper given at the Summer Institute on Teacher Education, Simon Fraser University, Vancouver, 1980; published in D. Hopkins and M. Wideen (eds.) *Alternative Perspectives on School Improvement* Falmer Press, 1984, pp. 67–76.

* 'Curriculum research and the art of the teacher': a paper given at the annual conference of the Association for the Study of the Curriculum, Brighton, 1980, and published in *Curriculum* 1, 1, Spring 1980, pp. 40–4.

Curriculum Research and Development in Action (editor) Heinemann Educational Books, 1980.

* Product or process? A reply to Brian Crittenden *New Education* 2, 1, 1980, pp. 137–40.

The study of samples and the study of cases *British Educational Research Journal* 6,1, 1980, pp. 1–6.

Applying research to education: one experience *Northern Ireland Council for Educational Research Information Bulletin* 15, January 1981, pp. 1–4.

Educational procedures and attitudinal objectives: a paradox (with Gajendra K. Verma) *Journal of Curriculum Studies* 13, 4, 1981, pp. 329–37.

Using case studies in library research *Social Science Information Studies* 1, 1981, pp. 221–30.

* What counts as research? *British Journal of Educational Studies* 29, 2, June 1981, pp. 103–14.

'The conduct, analysis and reporting of case study in educational research and evaluation' in R. McCormick (ed.) *Calling Education to Account*, Heinemann Educational Books in association with the Open University, 1982, pp. 261–73.

'Curriculum and the quality of schooling': a paper given at Goldsmith's College Annual Conference, March 1982 and printed in the conference proceedings.

* 'The curriculum as hypothetical' 1982. Abstract of a paper that Lawrence Stenhouse was to have given at the 1983 American Educational Research Association Conference. (Unpublished.)

* 'Developing curriculum on the process model': a paper given at Sheffield Polytechnic, June 1982. (Unpublished.)

* *Teaching about Race Relations: Problems and Effects* (with G.K. Verma, R.D. Wild and J. Nixon) Routledge & Kegan Paul, 1982.

* 'A note on case study and educational practice': a paper given at a conference at Whitelands College, London, July 1982 and published in R.G. Burgess (ed.) *Field Methods in the Study of Education*, Falmer Press, 1984, pp. 211–33.

* *Authority, Education and Emancipation* Heinemann Educational Books, 1983.

'The legacy of the curriculum development movement' in M. Galton and B. Moon (eds.) *Changing Schools . . . Changing Curriculum* Harper and Row, 1983, pp. 347–55.

The relevance of practice to theory, *Theory into Practice* XXII, 3, Summer 1983, pp. 211–15.

* 'Evaluating curriculum evaluation' in C. Adelman (ed.) *The Politics and Ethics of Educational Evaluation* Croom Helm, 1984, pp. 77–86.